Convoy Ambush Case Studies

Richard E. Killblane

Transportation Corps Historian

<u>Contents</u>

Introduction

When the enemy adopts a policy to attack convoys, truck drivers become front line troops. Convoy commanders must then become tacticians.

Tactics is not something a student of war can expect to learn by reading a manual. There is no one answer to every question. Each problem requires its own solution. Certain principles, however, remain consistent through out each problem. The student of war must understand the difference. This concept of war is so vague and elusive that a great number of military philosophers have tried to articulate it into a concept that student can understand.

Because it varies from situation to situation tactics is not a doctrine. War is chaos. Simply put, in combat each side makes mistakes. The side that protects its weaknesses and exploits the enemy's wins. For the infantry, tactics is not a study of battlefield formations and maneuvers but doing whatever is necessary to bring all ones weapons to bear against a weak spot in the enemy position and exploiting it. It should not be much different with convoys. Most victories are determined at one decisive point in the battle. Winners train to make this a habit.

METT is probably the best way to understand tactics. While the mission of the infantry is to close with and destroy the enemy, the mission of the transportation corps is to deliver the cargo. The destruction of the enemy facilitates this mission but does not become the mission. A tactician has to think like a hunter. A successful hunter thinks like his prey. A tactician has to think like his enemy. Only by understanding how his enemy thinks can the tactician predict his enemy's next moves. By anticipating what the enemy will do next, and then the tactician can plan to exploit the vulnerabilities of his enemy. Through thorough knowledge of his own troops, the tactician can defend his weaknesses and apply his strengths to the enemy weaknesses. The tactician must constantly be aware of the terrain and how it provides an advantage to the enemy and how he might use it to his advantage.

However, there are too many uncertainties in combat. A tactician must be flexible just as a fighter. A fighter trains his body to move a certain way. These would be the equivalent of battle drills. He studies his opponent. He looks for patterns so he might predict where his opponent might leave himself open. He also looks at the opponent's strength, which he then plans to nullify or avoid. Kind of like a study of operational art, the fighter studies his opponent's strengths and weaknesses then plans to protect his weakness and match his own strength against his opponent's weakness. If it was that simple the fight would be over quick. Combat is not that simple. The opponent has also done his own study.

In an academic discussion with a martial artist, they can pint out every counter that would defeat any technique one might use against them. One can not defeat a martial artist in a discussion though. It is done in a fight. A boxer has only three punches, the straight, the hook or cross and the upper cut. With just these three punches, they win fights. The oriental martial arts has a multitude of punches and kicks each designed to strike a specific weak spot on the body, but in a fairly even contest, the basic usually determine the outcome. Timing is what separates the winners from the losers. The fighter wins by feel. He goes through his reputua of punches and combinations until in a flash he sees and opening and instinctively strikes at it with his strongest punch. The time that elapses between thought and action is almost instantaneous because of training. Connecting with the right punch determines a knockout.

To master the art of war, the tactician must train his mind and body just as a fighter. The tactician trains his mind through an academic study. For a warrior leader, the commander represents the head and the organization represents the body. He should train his organization as a fight trains his body. Battle drills or immediate reaction drills represents the building blocks of tactics. Like a fighter trains to perfect the punch or kick, the professional warrior trains his organization to perform its drill with the same level of perfection instantaneously. With the battle drills in place, the tactician then spars with an opponent in war games to bring the mind and body together.

How to study war? The student of tactics studies previous fights and mentally places himself in the position of the participants. Knowing what they knew, how would he have reacted? In hind sight, what was the best course of action, remembering that there is no one perfect solution? Any number of actions would have succeeded. The tactician must learn what would have worked best for him.

For this reason, I have pulled together all the examples of convoy ambushes. The 19th century, Vietnam War, and current war in Iraq provide a wealth of examples of convoy ambushes from which to study. Unfortunately, the US Army did not record many good accounts of ambushes during the Vietnam War. Much of what is presented in this text is based upon oral interviews of the participants, sometimes backed by official record, citations or reports. For this reason, some of the ambush case studies present only the perspective of a crew member of a gun truck or the convoy commander. Since this academic study works best when one mentally takes the place of one of the participants, this view of the ambush serves a useful purpose. After my own review of the ambushes, I have drawn my own conclusion as to what principles apply to convoy ambushes.

Vietnam War

1. Northern II Corps Tactical Zone

8th Transportation Group

The 8th Transportation Group had three truck battalions that hauled cargo back and forth along Route (QL) 19 through the Central Highlands. The 27th Transportation Battalion consisted of primarily medium trucks, M52 tractors pulling M126 trailers. The 54th Transportation Battalion had the light trucks, M54 5-ton and M35 2 ½-ton cargo trucks. Both of these battalions were garrisoned in the vicinity of Qui Nhon and marshaled at Cha Rang Valley every morning for the long haul to Pleiku, 110 miles to the west. The 124th Transportation Battalion had both light and medium truck companies which picked up cargo at Qui Nhon or pushed it out to the camps along the Cambodian border.

By September 1967, Route 19 was a two-lane unimproved road that ran about 35 miles along the coastal plain then snaked up a mountain to the An Khe Pass. At one point below this pass, the road switched back on itself in a sharp turn the drivers called "The Devil's Hairpin" or "Hairpin" for short. Traffic generally slowed to a crawl of 4 miles per hour at that turn regardless of whether the convoys were heading up hill or down. Once over the pass, the road leveled out but pot holes as deep as a foot kept traffic to 15 miles per hour. Right before Pleiku, the road again rose up to meet Mang Giang Pass then leveled out onto the Highland Plateau where their destination awaited.

Tanks and APCs provided convoy security at a series of check points along Route 19. The Korean Tiger Division had responsibility for the first eight check points at the bridges from Qui Nhon to the base of mountain. All the Korean soldiers had lived through the Korean War, 1950-53, and hated communists. They welcomed the opportunity to fight them anywhere. They were extremely professional and were proud to serve in Vietnam. Their method of responding to enemy resistance was brutal and often times involved civilians in the villages where the attacks occurred. Consequently, the enemy did not launch many attacks in the Republic of Korea (ROK) sector and the drivers felt safe. However, the Koreans did not guard the slope leading up to An Khe Pass.

Up until September 1967, there were no convoy ambushes other than occasional sniping or planting of mines in the road. For that reason, convoy commanders did not concern themselves with interval between vehicles in the mountains. More often, the faster trucks pulled up bumper-to-bumper and pushed the slower trucks in front of them when going up hill. It was not uncommon to see a number of trucks driving in tandem. The 8th Group usually kicked out two convoy serials of 30 to 40 vehicles early in the morning. Convoys were generally grouped by type of trucks; light truck convoys fell under the control of a 54th Battalion convoy commander and the medium trucks fell under the 27th. Within each serial, trucks were generally arranged by load; the heavier or more explosive loads like fuel and projectiles in the rear.

Convoys kicked out early in the morning usually reaching Pleiku by noon. After either unloading their cargo or switching trailers, they returned that afternoon reaching Cha

Rang Valley by dark. Convoys did not run along Route 19 at night, so there was only one run made a day.

The battalions had SOPs for reaction to ambushes but since they had not encountered any, most soldiers did not know what their doctrine was. The 54th Battalion had been in Vietnam since October the year before. Major Nicholas Collins, 54th Battalion S-3, had consulted with other truck and infantry units as to an appropriate reaction to any particular threat. The popular consensus that ended up in the SOP read, "If caught in an ambush, halt in the center of road (shoulders may be mined). Take cover and return fire in the direction of the enemy, and be prepared to assault the enemy position and to fight your way out." At that time, the drivers of 8th Group were armed with the M14 rifle instead of the shorter M16. Since the doctrine was to dismount the vehicle and return fire, the length of the weapon was immaterial.

One of the companies of the 54th, the 666th Light Truck, had recently arrived that August. It had been assigned to Fort Benning, Georgia, where it supported the US Army Ranger School among other duties. The drivers were probably the only drivers in the 8th Group who had any reaction to ambush training.

2 September 1967

54th Transportation Battalion

On 2 September, the North Vietnamese Army (NVA) changed their tactics. They found the weakness to the American air assault concept. Realizing that the combat forces at An Khe and Pleiku were entirely dependent upon trucks for supplies, the NVA attacked the supply line.

An eastbound convoy of 90 trucks from both battalions was returning that afternoon from Pleiku under the protection of only two jeeps. The 54th Battalion had control of lead serial of 37 cargo trucks, which consisted of trucks from its different companies. Because of mechanical problems, a 5,000-gallon tanker split the serial in two as it approached the treacherous An Khe Pass between Check Points 89 and 96. At that time the jungle grew right up to the road, so close that the driver could reach out and touch the branches.[1]

At 1855 hours that evening, an NVA company struck the lead gun jeep with a 57mm recoilless rifle round killing SGT Leroy Collins and wounding the driver and gunner. Simultaneously, the enemy sprung a secondary ambush on the other half of the convoy setting the tanker on fire. The enemy was dug in on the hill above of the road firing down on the trucks. [2]

J.D. Calhoun, of the 666th, was driving his 2 ½-ton truck eighth in line of march. He barely heard the firing of small arms over the roar of his diesel engines. Calhoun did not realize that he was in an ambush until he saw the impact of bullets on the truck ahead of

[1] Colonel Joe O. Bellino, "8th Transportation Group; Sep 1967 – Sep 1968." n.d and Interview with Phillip C. Brown and J.D. Calhoun by Richard Killblane, 13 June 2003.

[2] Bellino, "8th Transportation" and Wolfe Interview.

him and came to a halt. He thought, "Oh crap. I can't sit in a truck. I've got to get out and get behind something." The drivers were taken by surprise. Many did not know what to expect. The kill zone spread out over 700 to 1,000 meters. There was no established policy at that time for reaction to a convoy ambush. The drivers of the Triple 6 had learned to get out of the trucks and return fire, but they had no other choice. The disabled trucks ahead of them blocked the road. Stopping turned out to be a bad idea. Drivers climbed out of their vehicles and returned fire while NVA swarmed over the trucks. J.D. jumped out and took cover between his truck and the hill side. A convoy halted in the kill zone was exactly what the enemy wanted. Since the drivers were support troops, they did not carry much ammunition. It quickly ran out.[3]

In ten minutes the enemy had destroyed or damaged 30 vehicles, killing seven men and wounding 17. The AC-47 gun ship, "Spooky" arrived at 2020 hours but the enemy had escaped under the cover of darkness. The 1st Cav pursued the enemy for about a week estimating that their strength around 60.[4]

This ambush sent shock waves throughout the 8th Group. For the truck drivers the nature of the war had changed. They had become the primary objective of the enemy offensive. From then on when they drove out the gate the drivers expected that they could be killed.

<u>NVA Lessons</u>

Their tactics had worked. Hitting an empty convoy returning from Pleiku did not shut down the supply line but only reduced the number of vehicles and drivers available for line haul. This had been a rehearsal. The enemy had deliberately planned the ambush for late that evening so they could escape under the cover of darkness. From their success and the US reaction, they developed their plans for future ambushes. For two years the NVA had sparred with the air cavalry only to learn to avoid American tactical air power. The speedy response of this tactical air power made the difference between the outcome of this ambush and the annihilation of French Mobile Group 100. The NVA would limit the duration of their ambushes to about 10 minutes which was short of the arrival of helicopters or the AC-47. The NVA would take two months to plan, rehearse and execute their next convoy ambush.

<u>US Lessons</u>

There was nothing obvious to predict that the enemy would change his tactics and target the convoys. An analyst might have drawn that conclusion by looking at the big picture. The insurgents had not any successes on the battlefield against the air assault units. He therefore had to find another weakness. The dependency on fuel hauled by trucks was a weakness. It was clearly known that this enemy was proficient at ambush tactics and had targeted convoys.

Surprise gave the enemy the advantage in the initiation of the ambush. After that it became a contest of the employment of fire power. LTC Melvin M. Wolfe came up with the idea in the summer of 1967 to experiment with gun trucks and LTC Philip N. Smiley,

---

3 Brown and Calhoun interview.

4 Bellino, "8th Transportation."

Commander of the 27th Battalion, built sandbag pill boxes on the back of two 2 ½-tons, which unfortunately were not in this convoy when it was hit. The only alternative to gun trucks was training the drivers to fight as infantry.

Since the enemy had begun targeting the convoys, they needed protection. The question was whether the protection was the responsibility of the combat unit which had responsibility for the area or the truck companies themselves. Complacency had set in. It was not a question of whether the SOP for reaction to an ambush was adequate as none of the drivers knew it. They had never had a need to. The 8th Transportation Group would have to look at both active and passive measures to protect the convoys.

Doctrine Change

External Action Taken

Within a week, LTG Stanley R. Larsen, Commander of I Field Force, Vietnam, held an informal meeting at the 1st Cavalry Division's Headquarters at An Khe. This was not to assess blame but to determine what measures should be taken to protect the convoys. Doctrinally, route security was the responsibility of the unit responsible for the area. As it turned out, everyone had become complacent. They reviewed each unit's responsibilities in reference to convoy security. Since the 1st Cavalry Division had most of its units in the field, it could not guard the road. Larsen instead ordered the 4th Infantry Division (Mechanized) at Pleiku to secure the road.[5]

They did so by setting up tanks and APCs at check points along the road. These check points were usually located at bridges and culverts or likely trouble spots. There were bridges and culverts about every three miles. From these check points the security forces could serve as reaction forces in the event of any nearby ambush. Neither the Koreans nor the Americans, however, could station mechanized troops in the most likely ambush locations in the mountain passes.[6]

In the event of an ambush, someone with a radio would call, "Contact, Contact, Contact" and all combat units in the area would be at the convoy's disposal. The 4th Infantry Division (Mechanized) had tanks and M113 armored personnel carriers stationed at check points along Route (QL) 19. These check points were generally posted at bridges or culverts where the enemy might place mines, generally every three miles in the level areas. In theory, the tanks and APCs could respond to any ambush in between them. However, there were none in the two mountain passes, An Khe and Mang Giang.

Since the security forces had responsibility for their section of the road, they had command and control of the convoys entering into their area of operations. They could stop the convoys if they detected trouble up ahead. They also passed on current enemy intelligence about the road. If a conflict arose between the convoy and the security force then the highway coordinator of the Traffic Management Agency would resolve it. This command and control relied on radio communication. Convoy briefings every morning

---

[5] COL (R) John Burke telephone interview by Richard Killblane, 30 March 2004 and COL (R) Melvin M. Wolfe telephone interview by Richard E. Killblane, 31 March and 14 April 2004.

[6] Burke and Wolfe interviews.

hopefully included the accurate radio frequencies of the security forces guarding the road. Convoy commanders had to call in and authenticate to the frequency of the next security force at the top of An Khe Pass. They soon ran out of range of their battalion headquarters when they passed over the mountains. They had to rely on the combat units to relay any messages back to battalion headquarters. They next authenticated to the frequency of the force at An Khe. There the convoy halted to drop of supplies destined for those units. The next frequency change was with the unit at Mang Giang and at last the convoy commander switched to the frequency of the force based at his destination at Pleiku.[7]

Larsen felt that the trucks should not have been out on the road at night. He ordered the road closed at 3:15 for eastbound traffic out of Pleiku and at 5:00 in the evening out of An Khe instead of 7:00. To depart on time, the convoys left Qui Nhon earlier. They rolled out the gate at 3:00 in the morning. The 815th Engineer Battalion also began clearing away the vegetation back 1,000 meters on both sides of the road with heavy grading equipment called "Rome Plows." This measure hoped to deny enemy the cover of the jungle to hide in.

The Military Police also provided route security. B Company, 504th Military Police Battalion cleared the road with two gun jeeps armed with M60 machineguns each morning from An Khe to Check Point 102 at Mang Giang Pass, then the gun jeeps of C Company, 504th would escort the convoys the rest of the way into Pleiku. The MPs would send an escort of two gun jeeps out. One would lead ahead of the convoy and the other would follow behind at a distance. Other than that, no combat vehicles would escort the convoys. On occasion, convoys could have access to occasional air support. When intelligence reports indicated likely enemy activity, an L-19 "Birddog" observation plane would fly surveillance over the area. After that meeting, both LTC Burke and Wolfe realized that their convoys still had to defend themselves.[8]

Internal Actions Taken

Internally, complacency had set in with the drivers of the 8th Group since no convoy had been ambushed during the first two years of the ground war. The first thing that LTC John Burke, acting 8th Group Commander, did after the ambush was read the standard operating procedures (SOP) and make any needed changes. As RMK paved the road toward Pleiku, the trucks could drive faster than 35 miles per hour. The official 8th Group SOP required convoys to obey speed limits and reduce speeds commensurate with road, weather and traffic conditions. It stated, "Speed generates carelessness." Speed limits through villages reduced to around 15 miles per hour. The truck drivers knew it was harder to hit a fast moving target. Some convoy commanders briefed that trucks should drive as fast as they could go.[9]

---

[7] Bellino, "8th Transportation."
[8] Burke and Wolfe interviews.
[9] MAJ Nicholas H. Collins, "Battalion S-3 Notes," Headquarters, 54th Transportation Battalion, APO 96238, 5 March 1967, Burke interview and Collins interviews.

It then became imperative that trucks maintain a 100 meter interval between trucks. This interval limited the number of trucks in the kill zone. Under these conditions, the 1,000 meter kill zone of the ambush on 2 September would have only caught ten trucks instead of 37. The ambushes occurred at places where traffic had to slow down. Drivers should also watch for changes in familiar scenes along the route. There were usually changes in behavior to indicate an ambush up ahead. The absence of people on the streets, the gathering of unusual looking people or even civilian vehicles parked along side the road waiting for the convoy to pass indicated that there was danger ahead. The locals knew very well what the enemy was up to in their area.[10]

In the event of an ambush, the thin skinned vehicles had to rapidly clear the kill zone. Truck drivers would not stop in an ambush for any reason even if wounded. Those that could drove out of the kill zone, those that could not turned around and drove back to the security of the nearest check point. If the vehicle was disabled then the driver should pull off to the side of the road, dismount and jump on a passing vehicle. If the disabled vehicle could not pull off to the side of the road, then the next vehicle would push it out of the way. If the task vehicles could not turn around then they would halt at 100 meter intervals, the drivers would dismount and provide security. From then on the convoy commander briefed these procedures every morning. However, these were just passive measures to limit vulnerability.[11]

<u>Gun Trucks</u>

LTC Burke then met with his battalion and company commanders to discuss what active measures the 8th Group could do to protect their convoys. Since they could not count on the combat arms units to protect them, they needed their offensive firepower. The 8th Group initially borrowed M-55s, Quad .50s mounted on M-35 2 ½-ton trucks, from the local artillery unit. The Quad .50 was four synchronized .50 caliber machineguns mounted on the bed of a 2 ½-ton truck. The Quad .50 gun trucks, however, required a crew of six, one driver the truck, one gunner and four men to reload each of the guns. The crews took their training from the artillery unit, which provided the weapons.[12]

Since each company had a few 2 ½-ton trucks for administrative duties, they converted them to gun trucks within weeks of the 2 September ambush. In World War II and Korean War, a gun truck was any truck with a ring mounted machinegun. As a task vehicle they could only return fire while fleeing the kill zone. The new 2 ½-ton gun trucks were built from precut steel platting that had been ordered during the summer. It arrived just after the 2 September ambush. The battalion commanders directed the construction of gun trucks; company commanders picked the crews and left the design to them. The crew consisted of a driver, NCOIC armed with an M-79 grenade launcher riding shotgun" in the passenger seat of the cab and two gunners with M-60 machineguns standing in the gun box. When ring mounts arrived, some crews added an M-2 .50 caliber to the cab. The new gun truck was a dedicated weapons platform which could maneuver to protect task vehicles.

---

[10] Bellino, "8th Transportation."
[11] Bellino, "8th Transportation."
[12] Burke interview.

The gun trucks were integral to the companies and the leaders appointed the crew members. Only a few crews had named their gun trucks at that time. That early in their development, they were very generic and had not taken on any character. The new SOP called for a gun truck ratio of one for every ten task vehicles. Their mission was to move to the flank of the kill zone and return fire on the enemy. Up until 24 November, the gun truck doctrine had not been tested in an enemy ambush.

The limitation of the gun truck was the availability of radios. Few trucks had them and then only one. Usually just the convoy commander and the assistant convoy commanders had radios so the gun trucks without radios had to watch them for instructions. With the proper intervals, long convoys could stretch for a mile and some gun jeeps and gun trucks may not hear the gun fire to respond.

Tet Offensive

The NVA commanding general, Vo Nguyen Giap, was confident that the conditions were ripe for the Viet Cong to rise up and join the invading NVA in the final phase of his insurgency strategy. The official commencement of offensive operations began on the night of 31 January 1968, the Vietnamese Lunar New Year celebration known as Tet. The NVA had agreed to a cease fire during the holiday so that the Army of the Republic of Vietnam (ARVN) soldiers could go home for the holidays. In effect, the NVA hoped to catch the ARVN completely off guard. The only force that could seriously contend his operations was the Americans.

Giap clearly understood the American dependence on supplies and knew that he had to sever the American supply line hoping to starve the combat units spread throughout the Central Highlands and Highland Plateau. For the 8th Transportation Group, the Tet Offensive began with a convoy ambush on 24 November 1967. From then on large scale convoy ambushes would become weekly occurrences with mining and sniping taking place daily. The objective of the enemy convoy attacks was to completely shut down the supply line.

24 November 1967

54th Transportation Battalion

It took the enemy usually a week to plan and rehearse large scale ambushes. The NVA launched its second large scale ambush on a 54th Battalion convoy led by 1LT James P. Purvis on 24 November 1967. The westbound convoy consisted of 43 5-ton cargo trucks, 15 2 ½-ton trucks and a maintenance truck under the protection of six gun trucks and three gun jeeps. It was divided into six serials of about ten task vehicles per serial and one gun trucks led each serial.[13]

Jerry Christopher rode shotgun in the cab of the lead 2 ½-ton gun truck which traveled 20 miles per hour down the road. At 1005 hours, he spotted ten paper bags spaced across the road and recognized them as fertilizer mines. He shouted to his driver, Bob Logston, "We're in the kill zone! "What?" Logston shouted over the roar of the engine. "We're in

---

[13] Bellino, "8th Transportation."

an ambush!" Logston floored the gas pedal and grabbed his rifle. The two machine gunners in the box opened fire with their M-60s. A B-40 rocket then slammed into the front end blowing off the left tire and part of the wheel. The gun truck slid to a halt 25 yards short of the mines. Christopher yelled into the radio had get, "Contact! Contact! Contact!" He tumbled out of the vehicle with Logston behind him and started firing his M-79 grenade launcher. Enemy fire ripped through the windshield, the engine block and into the armor plating on the side of the cab.[14]

The SOP for an ambush was for those vehicles in the 300-meter long kill zone to not stop but drive out. The next 5-ton loaded with small arms ammunition, down shifted, pulled out of line and roared around the damaged gun truck unaware of the daisy chain ahead. The mines blew off the front end and the truck swerved out of control off to the right side of the road. The third driver also accelerated his rig and ran over the remaining mines loosing both front wheels. His truck slid 75 yards down the road and ended up in a ditch across the road with his load of 155mm high explosive projectiles on fire. SP4 Dick Dominquez revved his engine and raced for the gap in the road. Carrying a load of CS gas, he safely squeezed through the gap and headed on to Pleiku. His was the only truck to escape the kill zone. The enemy hit the next truck loaded 155mm projectiles with a B-40 rocket and set it on fire. It slid to a halt 50 yards from Christopher's gun truck. Route 19 was completely blocked by damaged vehicles.[15]

Christopher began firing his grenade launcher at the suspected position of the B-40. The artillery ammunition load began to cook off. Each blast rocked the corpse of the gun truck near it. Christopher crawled to the front of the vehicle looking for his driver. Logston had been hit by machine gun fire below the waist and was a bloody mess. He was trying to crawl out of the firing line. Christopher called out, "Bob! Y'all right, Bob?" Christopher then pulled his driver into the elephant grass. Jerry asked, "What're we gonna do now, Jerry?" He looked up and saw helicopters circling high above. "Why don't they do something? Why don't they help us?" These were command and control bird with senior officers. Christopher pulled Jerry under the gun truck and bandaged his wounds. "Hang on – we'll make it OK." That was as much his wish as reassurance.[16]

Another rocket hit the tail gate above Christopher sending a shower of fragments all over SP4 Czerwinsky, a machine gunner. The other machine gunner, Jim Boyd, was hit in the arm. Both M-60 machine guns were smashed. While Christopher tried to save Czerwinsky's life, Boyd searched for a rifle and started firing away with his good arm. Christopher then saw an NVA sapper in the grass across the road. He fired with his M-79 not sure if there was enough distance for the round to arm. The round exploded on target.[17]

When the ambush began, a B-40 rocket passed just inches behind the next gun truck, seventeenth vehicle in the serial. Machine gunners, Roy Handers and Bob Sas, opened

[14] Ibid.
[15] Ibid.
[16] Ibid.
[17] Ibid.

fire. The next rocket hit the cab, wounding the driver and throwing him to the floor boards. The truck lumbered out of control off the side of the road. When the truck hit the ditch it flipped over throwing the crew around inside the box. The truck stopped upside down in the grass. Handers found himself pinned under the truck by his leg. Sas was crushed to death under the cab. Handers could hear the driver trapped in the cab crying for help. Handers dug himself free with his hands only to find that his leg was broken. An NVA machine gunner on the other side of the vehicle kept him from helping to the driver. He crawled around looking for a weapon when he heard a "plop" beside him. The grenade went off and blew him ten feet away. With fragments in his legs, he staggered to his feet and tried to get back to the truck when he blacked out.[18]

5,000-gallon fuel tankers in the first serial had burst into flames spilling their flaming contents down the road for 700 yards. Pallets of ammunition on the backs of the other trucks began to cook off. NVA sappers ran up to the vehicles, climbed atop and placed demolition charges on the cargo then fired down on the drivers hiding in the grass along the side of the road. Drivers returned fire knocking the enemy off of their trucks into the wreckage littering the road.[19]

Enemy fire also hit the gun truck in the third serial and damaged it. A grenade damaged the gun truck in the fourth serial. Only the last two gun trucks remained undamaged. The drivers and the gun trucks fought back fixing the enemy in place while tanks and APCs of the 4th Infantry Division at Check Point 91 West came up and flanked the enemy. The enemy had damaged 14 trucks to include four gun trucks, killed two drivers, SP4 Arthur J. Hensinger and PFC Robert Sas, and wounded 17 at a loss of 41 of their own killed and four captured wounded.[20]

Lessons

Clearly the gun trucks caught the enemy by surprise. Assaulting the convoy as they had before made them pay a high price, yet the convoy also sustained high losses. The NVA would not be so reckless the next time. They would conduct convoy ambushes nearly every week and test the capabilities of the gun trucks. With a limited arsenal of weapons available, the enemy would vary his tactics trying to determine what weapons to initiate with, how large should the kill zone be and what vehicles to destroy first.

In spite of armor at check points, the enemy would conduct ambushes at the areas not covered, most likely in the mountain passes. The slope below Mang Giang Pass would become known over the next few months as "Ambush Alley." An Khe Pass would be the next favorite ambush area. During the last two convoy ambushes, he had initiated the ambush on the lead vehicles.

The 8th Group, however, was on the right path to a solution. An ambush is a quick and violent attack that relies on surprise to be effective. The gun trucks would learn that they needed to turn the fight around fast with greater violence. The gun trucks needed more

[18] Ibid.
[19] Ibid.
[20] Ibid.

fire power. While the Quad .50s had far superior fire power, each of the four guns required a loader. This required a crew of six; a driver, a gunner and four loaders, far more than the truck companies could afford. The Quad .50s would soon fall from the inventory. The box style gun trucks began to mount M2 .50 caliber machineguns either on ring mounts over the cab or on pedestals in the gun box. The 7.62mm rounds of the M60 did not have the penetrating ability of the .50 caliber. Eventually, three machineguns became standard for each gun truck.

Not having radios in each truck prevented the lead gun truck from warning the others of the mines across the road. The radio call, "Contact, contact, contact" was an alert for external support.

4 December 1967

54th Transportation Battalion

Another eastbound convoy returned from Pleiku under the control of the 54th Battalion was ambushed by a company of Viet Cong guerrillas at 0815 hours on the morning of 4 December. This convoy of 58 5-ton trucks, 11 2 ½-ton trucks was escorted by six gun trucks, four gun jeeps and a maintenance truck. 1LT Todd, the convoy commander, rode in the lead gun jeep behind a gun truck.[21]

The lead gun truck, from the 669th Transportation Company, stopped west of An Khe when the crew noticed a board with three mines pulled across the road. The gun truck then received small arms fire and a direct hit from a recoilless rocket in the windshield killing the driver, Specialist Four Harold Cummings, and wounding the crew in the gun box, SGT Dennis Belcastro, Frank Giroux and Joe Foster. The crews of the gun truck and gun jeep returned fire. Five minutes after the ambush started the enemy made a strike at the center of the convoy. Four cargo trucks received flat tires but the drivers returned fire breaking off the assault. Three minutes later the enemy made another assault, which was also beaten back.[22]

The remaining five gun trucks raced into the 3,000 meter long kill zone multiplying the suppressive fire on the enemy. One was disabled by a rocket, which wounded the three gunners. The helicopter gun ships arrived at 0827 hours, 12 minutes after the call, "ambush, ambush, ambush" went out and the reaction force arrived at 0830 hours. By that time the gun trucks had broken up the enemy ambush, killing 13 enemy soldiers and capturing one wounded at a loss of only one American killed and six wounded. The loss of vehicles was one gun truck destroyed and one jeep and four trucks slightly damaged.[23]

Lesson

This time the gun trucks did not try to run through the kill zone but stopped to fight. Although wounded, the three machine gunners and drivers of the cargo trucks managed to lay down enough fire to beat back two enemy attacks until the gun trucks from behind

[21] Bellino, "8th Transportation."
[22] Bellino, "8th Transportation."
[23] Bellino, "8th Transportation."

came up to increase the fire power. This action reduced the number of vehicles destroyed or damaged and increased the number of enemy casualties.

The enemy had initiated the last two ambushes with a daisy chain of mines pulled across the road instead of destroying the lead vehicle with rockets. The truck companies had not anticipated this. Clearly the mines had prevented the drivers from clearing the kill zone as their SOP called for. Later, the gunners of the gun trucks learned to fire their machineguns at anything suspicious along the road. They preferred this to firing the grenade launcher or rocket from the Light Anti-tank Weapon (LAW) as the latter would definitely set off an explosion but not always detonate the mines. The tracer rounds of the machineguns could set off the mines and the secondary explosions would let the drivers know the path was clear.

21 January 1968

54th Transportation Battalion

At approximately 0615 hours on 21 January 1968, a convoy under the control of the 54th Battalion consisting of 60 cargo trucks, four gun trucks and four gun jeeps departed Qui Nhon for Pleiku.[24]

Again the enemy placed mines in the road. The convoy was halted at Check Point 96 East for 30 minutes while the road was cleared. At 1000 hours, approximately 500 yards east of Check Point 102, below Mang Giang Pass, the lead element of the convoy came upon a 5-ton tractor which was attempting to hook up to a 5,000-gallon fuel trailer. Because this operation blocked the flow of traffic, the convoy commander drove forward and directed the clearance of the road. He then instructed his convoy to continue. At this time, the enemy opened fire with automatic and small arms on the south side of the road. Gun trucks and gun jeeps immediately returned fire while the rest of the convoy continued to drive through the kill zone. Within five to ten minutes APCs from the road security element at Check Point 102 arrived and engaged the enemy. Tanks from Check Point 98 arrived within ten minutes. Rear elements of the convoy approaching the area received approximately 40 to 50 rounds of automatic fire. Both APCs and tanks at the site of the incident fired in the direction of the hostile fire.[25]

Lesson

This ambush was more likely a hasty ambush using only small arms fire. Here the SOPs worked. The gun trucks placed suppressive fire on the enemy so the convoy could clear the kill zone. The security force then responded to the kill zone but after the truck had cleared it.

25 January 1968

54th Transportation Battalion

At 0600 hours on 25 January 1968, a convoy under the control of the 54th Battalion consisting of 95 vehicles destined for Pleiku and 23 for An Khe departed the marshalling area a Cha Rang Valley. The 95 vehicles bound for Pleiku consisted of 65 5-ton cargo

---

[24] Bellino, "8th Transportation."

[25] Bellino, "8th Transportation."

trucks; 19 2 ½-ton cargo trucks; five 2 ½-ton gun trucks, four radio gun jeeps and two 5-ton maintenance trucks.[26]

At approximately, 1015 hours, the convoy received automatic and small arms fire from both sides of the road at BR 089552. The gun trucks and convoy personnel returned fire and within 10 minutes elements of the 2/1 Cavalry arrived with APCs and tanks. After all the firing stopped, the convoy proceeded west for approximately 500 yards when the convoy again came under fire. The NVA opened fire on the second and third vehicles in the convoy with rockets, heavy machineguns, grenades and small arms fire from both sides of the road. A machinegun position was later discovered approximately 25 yards from the right side of the road. The reaction force arrived from the previous ambush site immediately. The kill zone spanned 1,000 meters from BR 089552 to BR 080550. Three armed helicopters arrived at approximately 1045 hours. Two medevac helicopters arrived within 10 minutes after receiving the request. Two officers, members of the engineer team, were wounded, one fatally, while clearing explosive ordnance from the site.[27]

Approximately 60 personnel from the convoy and the reaction force were involved in the ambush. The number of enemy personnel involved was unknown. Two drivers were killed and one wounded. One 2 ½-ton gun truck and one 2 ½-ton truck were damaged, with minor damage to the cargo. One civilian tractor form the Pacific Architects and Engineers (PAE) was destroyed.[28]

Lesson

The enemy had changed his tactics again. Evidently the enemy had studied the gun truck tactics. They had noticed that the gun trucks stayed in the kill zone while the task vehicles escaped. The enemy may have planned the first ambush as a decoy to draw off the gun trucks hoping that the unprotected trucks escaping the first kill zone would drive into the main kill zone. In this case, the gun trucks defended the halted convoy long enough for the reaction force to arrive then left. This placed the reaction force only a short distance behind the convoy when it drove through the next kill zone. This allowed the armored cavalry to respond rapidly and turn the fire back on the enemy.

The enemy watches for patterns. Varying tactics can set the enemy up for failure. Some gun trucks should remain with the vehicles that escape the kill zone and having a combat arms force following a close distance behind but out of sight of the convoy provides a great tactical surprise for the enemy that ambushes the convoy.

30 January 1968

54th Transportation Battalion

On 30 January 1968, a convoy under the control of the 54th Battalion departed for Pleiku at approximately 0600 hours that morning. The convoy consisted of 80 cargo trucks,

[26] Bellino, "8th Transportation."
[27] Bellino, "8th Transportation."
[28] Bellino, "8th Transportation."

seven gun trucks, eight gun jeeps and three Quad .50s. This exceeded the 1:10 ratio of gun trucks to prime movers.[29]

Upon arrival in An Khe, the convoy was joined by three APCs and one tank from the security force of the 173rd Airborne Brigade. The additional security element was dispersed toward the front of the convoy. Since the convoy was about to pass out of the area of operation of the 173rd, the additional security element pulled out of the convoy and stopped at Check Point 102 (BR 253483). Approximately one mile west of Check Point 102, the convoy came under enemy fire initially from mortars followed by small arms and automatic fire from a platoon-size enemy force. The convoy personnel immediately returned fire. In addition, the 173rd Airborne Brigade security element advanced from Check Point 102 and an element for the 4th Infantry Division security element moved west to engage the enemy. F111As, F104s and helicopter gun ships made air strikes. Two US personnel were slightly injured, one 5-ton tractor and reefer were damaged. No enemy dead or wounded were found.[30]

Lesson

In this case the role of the security force was much more proactive. Their presence along with the high number of gun trucks suppressed the enemy attack minimizing any damage to vehicles or casualties.

31 January 1968

124th Transportation Battalion

1 February was the Lunar New Year or Tet, one of the most popular holidays in Vietnam. It is like Christmas and New Years rolled into one holiday. The insurgents had agreed to a ceasefire so that the Army of the Republic of Vietnam (ARVN) soldiers could go home for the holidays. On 31 January 1968, the enemy launched a nationwide offensive.[31]

That day, 1LT David R. Wilson, 64th Medium Truck Company, led a convoy from Pleiku to An Khe. The convoy consisted of 24 5-ton tractor-trailer combinations, two radio equipped gun jeeps and three 2 ½-ton gun trucks from the 124th Battalion. Seven 5-ton cargo trucks, with a lead 2 ½-ton gun truck and trail radio equipped gun jeep from the 54th Battalion made up the rear of the convoy. Two Quad .50 gun trucks attached from B Battery, 4th Battalion, 60 Field Artillery accompanied the convoy. The loads consisted of four 5,000-gallon fuel tankers, two Class II and IV loads, five Class IV loads and eight Class V (ammunition) loads. The trucks from the 54th Battalion hauled engineer Class IV loads. Wilson employed a convoy line up of gun jeeps front and rear with gun trucks evenly spaced throughout the convoy. He placed the Quad .50s in the middle of the convoy. At that time convoy commanders rode in the front of the convoy either in front of or behind the lead gun truck.[32]

---

[29] Bellino, "8th Transportation."

[30] Bellino, "8th Transportation."

[31] Bellino, "8th Transportation."

[32] Bellino, "8th Transportation."

The convoy made it safely to An Khe and departed for the return trip at 1430 hours. On the return trip, the convoy reached the base of the Mang Giang Pass. Where the road grade started to raise slightly, the area was cleared for approximately 100 yards on both sides of the road. This stretch of road where the French Mobile Group 100 was destroyed and the site of recent ambushes became known as "Ambush Alley." At 1520 hours, the lead vehicles started up the pass when the enemy initiated the ambush with mortars on the middle of the convoy, in the vicinity of grid coordinates BR 252483. The enemy was halfway up the pass located in the wood line.[33]

The lead gun truck escorted the lead elements of the convoy to the top of the Pass in accordance with the SOP. However, many of the vehicles behind him had halted in the kill zone and were subject to an intense enemy mortar and small arms fire. Upon hearing the firing behind him, 1LT Wilson, immediately ordered his driver, SP4 Brammer, to turn the jeep around and reenter the kill zone to make an estimate of the situation and so he could insure the safe passage of the rear element of the convoy. Wilson's gunner, SP4 Earnest W. Fowlke, blazed away with the M-60. Upon reaching the edge of the kill zone, he saw that the enemy fired small arms, automatic weapons, 60mm and 82mm mortars into a 400 yard long kill zone. Wilson then turned the jeep around and headed back up the Pass. The jeep had traveled 50 yards when a mortar round hit it causing it to burst into flames, killing Wilson instantly and mortally wounding Fowlke. Brammer was only slightly wounded. The burning jeep rolled into a ditch.[34]

Once the lead element of the convoy was safely up the Pass, the lead gun truck returned to the kill zone. As it came down the Pass, the two machine gunners, SP4 Howell and SP4 Bushong, saw the two Quad .50s racing up the Pass to safety. One driver said they only saw one return fire as it beat other trucks out of the kill zone. The 2 ½-tn gun truck stopped at the edge of the kill zone. The middle gun truck raced up to a position about 50 yards from the first. To obtain better fields of fire and maximum coverage, the gun trucks remained in the kill zone.[35]

The last gun truck of the 124th Battalion headed up the road but was stopped by MPs at Check Point 102. Evidently unaware of the ambush the driver, SP5 Jimmie Jackson, jumped out to find out why the convoy had stopped. None of the gun trucks had radios. Then the rear gun jeep arrived with SGT Welch, PFC Jimmy Tidwell and PFC Cansans. PFC Tidwell informed Jackson and the security force that the convoy up ahead was ambushed. Tidwell jumped into the driver's seat of the gun truck and Jackson climbed in the gun box to man a machine gun. They drove up to Wilson's burning jeep and returned fire on the enemy. They remained in position until the MPs instructed the convoy to move forward. Jackson and SP4 Green were wounded in the fight. Only Wilson's jeep was destroyed.[36]

---

[33] Bellino, "8th Transportation."
[34] Bellino, "8th Transportation."
[35] Bellino, "8th Transportation."
[36] Bellino, "8th Transportation."

There were two APCs and one tank in the area. Helicopter support did not arrive for 20 minutes.

Lesson

The enemy had changed his tactics. This and the ambush the day before were the first use mortars in a convoy ambush. The enemy also launched the ambush on the middle of the convoy instead of the front as it had in the past. This allowed the convoy commander and lead gun truck to escape. However, at great risk to life, 1LT Wilson and his crew drove back into the kill zone to save the lives of their drivers. For their personal bravery and sacrifice, 1LT Wilson and SP4 Fowlke were posthumously awarded the Silver Star Medals. The 124th Battalion named their camp after Wilson. While extremely brave, driving into a kill zone in an unarmored vehicle was dangerous.

By attacking the middle of the convoy, this split the convoy up. The lead vehicles drove on to safety while the vehicles behind the kill zone halted awaiting a decision. As the enemy increasingly began to attack the middle or rear of the convoys, convoy commanders realized that the front was not the place to be if they wanted to influence the action. The key decisions had to be made either in or behind the kill zone. For that reason, convoy commanders would learn to ride in the rear of the convoys.

The lack of radios in the gun trucks caused confusion in the rear when the MPs stopped the last gun truck. Without knowing what was happening ahead of them and with no communication with the convoy commander, the last gun truck was unable to respond in a timely manner.

Everyone needs to know what to do in an ambush, especially attachments. Besides being critical of the performance of the artillerymen in the Quad .50s, the truck drivers were disappointed with the delayed arrival of the helicopters. The machineguns on the gun trucks were effective weapons against other direct fire weapons but not against mortars hidden in the woods. Helicopters could more effectively spot the mortars which either they or artillery could then destroy. Similarly the MPs at the check point only knew to prevent vehicles from entering the kill zone. While it may have seemed obvious that the gun trucks should have been allowed through, fear causes a form of paralysis and Soldiers do only what they know.

7 February 1968

54th Transportation Battalion

On 7 February 1968, a convoy of 67 cargo trucks, six gun trucks, four gun jeeps and one maintenance truck under the control of the 54th Battalion departed Cha Rang Valley at 0630 hours. At approximately 1010 hours, after passing Check Point 92 (vicinity AR 9855503), the convoy came under small arms and automatic fire from 50 to 60 enemy soldiers in the tree line south of the road. In addition, two rockets were fired at the convoy from a mound halfway between the road and the tree line. One rocket hit a truck carrying a load of Class V (ammunition) and was destroyed. The enemy force then began to advance from the tree line but was driven back by the fire power of the convoy. The gun trucks, which had cleared the 200 meter long kill zone, returned to fire on the enemy positions. Within 15 minutes, six to eight APCs and two to three tanks arrived on the scene to engage the enemy. The helicopter gun ships arrived within 15 to 20 minutes.[37]

The Americans only had four men slightly wounded, but the enemy lost six killed and one wounded. Besides the one truck destroyed by the rocket, a 5-ton cargo truck had its gas tank damaged and many of the vehicles including the gun trucks received flat tires from enemy fire.[38]

13 February 1968

124th Transportation Battalion

On 13 February, a westbound convoy of 28 task vehicles, one maintenance vehicle, two gun jeeps, three gun trucks and three Quad .50s under the control of the 124th Battalion departed An Khe at 1335 hours. Around 1500 hours, 200 yards west of the base of the Mang Giang Pass (vicinity BR 237500), the enemy ambushed the lead elements of the convoy with mortars and small arms. The convoy personnel and gun trucks immediately returned fire. The convoy commander drove the convoy through the kill zone and directed one of the Quad .50s from the 4th Battalion, 60 Field Artillery to fire on the suspected enemy mortar position (vicinity BT 232495). The security forces of the 173rd Airborne Division arrived and attacked the enemy within 10 minutes. Air strikes were conducted against the suspected mortar positions. The enemy had only fired seven mortar rounds and caused no vehicle damage or wounded any drivers.[39]

Lesson

Gun truck tactics were significantly reducing casualties. The air power seemed to effectively counter the enemy mortar fire.

21 February 1968

27th Transportation Battalion

At approximately 0715 hours, 21 February, a convoy under the control of the 27th Battalion departed the marshalling yard at Cha Rang Valley for Pleiku. The convoy consisted of 54 task vehicles, four gun trucks, four gun jeeps and a Quad .50.[40]

At approximately 0950 hours, the convoy came under fire from automatic and small arms fire and B40 rockets between Check Point 89 and Check Point 96. The convoy personnel returned fire in the direction of an estimated 10 to 12 NVA south of the highway. The Quad .50 moved into the small kill zone, which was estimated at approximately 300 meters in length, and was credited with killing one NVA soldier. APCs from the 173rd Airborne Brigade arrived approximately five to 10 minutes after the call and engaged the enemy force. The tactical force also called in artillery. Three vehicles including a task vehicle and the Quad .50 were damaged and three personnel were wounded. One killed and one wounded enemy was recovered along with the discovery of numerous foxholes.[41]

---

[37] Bellino, "8th Transportation."

[38] Bellino, "8th Transportation."

[39] Bellino, "8th Transportation."

[40] Bellino, "8th Transportation."

[41] Bellino, "8th Transportation."

4 March 1968

54th Transportation Battalion

On 4 March, a convoy under the control of the 54th Battalion departed Cha Rang Valley for Pleiku at approximately 0600 hours. The convoy consisted of 104 task vehicles, 8 gun trucks and 4 gun jeeps.[42]

At approximately 0900 hours, the convoy was held up at Check Point 89 by the tactical security force due to enemy activity in Mang Giang Pass. The convoy was allowed to proceed at approximately 1130 hours with the escort of one tank and two APCs from the 173rd Airborne Brigade. At approximately 1145 hours, the convoy came under fire from mortars and heavy small arms and automatic fire. Convoy security immediately opened fire in the direction of the enemy which was well entrenched in the tree line on the north side of the road. The convoy also received sporadic fire from the south side of the road. The enemy force was estimated at about 50 personnel. Two Quad .50s from the 4th Battalion, 60th Artillery, which were traveling with the convoy, and one from the 27th Transportation Battalion convoy serial, which followed behind the 54th convoy, fired upon the enemy positions throughout the kill zone, estimated to be between 500 and a 1,000 meter long. A reaction force of one tank, four APCs and four gun ships arrived within five minutes.[43]

Eight convoy personnel were wounded, two from the artillery unit. One wounded died on 6 March, from wounds received in the battle. Five of the vehicles and two trailers were damaged. The convoy remained in place on the highway until 2:30, at which time they turned around under the escort of MPs and returned to An Khe.[44]

8 March 1968

54th Transportation Battalion

On 8 March, another 54th Battalion convoy had departed from Cha Rang Valley for Pleiku at approximately 0600 hours. The convoy consisted of 79 task vehicles, four gun jeeps and five gun trucks.[45]

At approximately 0830 hours, the third gun truck of the first serial was hit with a claymore mine damaging the front tires. The explosion was followed by heavy small arms and automatic fire from both sides of the road. Three Quad .50s from the 4th Battalion, 60th Artillery traveling with the convoy joined by a company of the 173rd Airborne Brigade, which was in the area, engaged the enemy. The company commander of the 173rd was killed during the engagement. The enemy force attempted to repel the flanking action of the tactical security force but was driven back after 15 minutes of heavy contact. One gun truck and one task vehicle were damaged. Two US personnel were wounded and one killed. One of the wounded was a driver and the other two were in the 173rd. The convoy was allowed to proceed after a twenty minute delay.[46]

---

[42] Bellino, "8th Transportation."
[43] Bellino, "8th Transportation."
[44] Bellino, "8th Transportation."
[45] Bellino, "8th Transportation."
[46] Bellino, "8th Transportation."

At approximately 0915 hours, two kilometers west of Check Point 102, a task vehicle in the first serial hit a mine then small arms fire hit the cab of the disabled vehicle wounding the driver. B40 rockets then ignited the JP4 that the truck hauled. Small arms and automatic fire and rockets opened up on the convoy in a kill zone of approximately 300-500 meters in length. The convoy security element fired in the direction of the enemy positions as the convoy maneuvered around the burning vehicle. Tactical security forces from the 173rd and the 4th ID arrived within five minutes and engaged the enemy. Only one soldier was wounded with one truck damaged and another destroyed. No enemy dead or wounded was recovered.[47]

Lesson

The enemy had again employed two kill zones. They also initiated the ambush on the gun trucks. The quick reaction by the gun trucks and security force reduced casualties.

16 March 1968

124th Transportation Battalion

On 16 March 1968, a convoy of 17 cargo trucks, three gun trucks, one gun jeep and a ¾-ton maintenance truck with an M-60 machinegun, under the control of 124th Battalion, departed Dak To for Pleiku on Route 14 at approximately 1430 hours. MPs from the 4th Infantry Division (Mechanized) escorted the convoy. The 124th Battalion pushed convoys of 2 ½-ton and 5-ton cargo trucks to the smaller base camps along the Cambodian border. Route 14 cut through dense jungle.[48]

At approximately 1800 hours the rear element of the convoy came under heavy small arms and automatic fire in the vicinity of ZA 195689 from a platoon size enemy force. The convoy personnel immediately returned fire in the direction of the enemy and moved rapidly out of the estimated 100 to 150 meter long kill zone. Tanks from the nearest tactical force arrived within three to five minutes and gun ships arrived within five to ten minutes. Only the maintenance vehicle in the rear was damaged and the machine gunner was killed.[49]

23 March 1968

Night Shuttle

On 23 March, a night shuttle convoy from the port of Qui Nhon was proceeding west on Highway 1 toward loading sites in Cha Rang Valley. Highway 1 was heavily trafficked by civilian traffic during the day and normally considered safe. Night convoys made the short run of about 8 miles from the port to the supply yards where loads would be prepared for the convoys the next morning.[50]

At approximately 0015 hours, the convoy consisting of five task vehicles, one gun truck and one gun jeep, approached the bridge guarded by the Koreans. The convoy commander, 1LT Paul J. Stegmayer, of 2nd Medium Truck, observed a pipe line fire in

[47] Bellino, "8th Transportation."
[48] Bellino, "8th Transportation."
[49] Bellino, "8th Transportation."
[50] Bellino, "8th Transportation."

the vicinity of Tuy Phovc. After reporting the same, 1LT Stegmayer proceeded with his column. As the convoy reached the site of the fire, an explosion occurred on the north side of the road near 1LT Stegmayer's jeep, followed by heavy small arms and automatic weapons fire. Although both 1LT Stegmayer and his driver received wounds from flying glass and shrapnel, they were able to cross over the bridge at the site of the pipe line fire. Due to the intense enemy fire, only the jeep and one task vehicle were able to clear the kill zone. Despite great personal danger, 1LT Stegmayer, braving a withering hail of bullets, crossed back over to bridge on foot to take control of the drivers and insure that they could clear the scene. Moving from vehicle to vehicle, Stegmayer assured himself that all drivers were out of their vehicles and had taken up positions to engage the enemy. He crossed back to his jeep to radio reports to Battalion and adjust illuminating artillery rounds.[51]

With arrival of a reaction force of three gun trucks, one gun jeep and a Quad .50, 1LT Stegmayer again crossed over the bridge to direct flanking fire into the suspected enemy positions. The enemy force estimated at 15 broke contact and fled the area. All six vehicles in the convoy received small arms and automatic weapons fire. Four personnel were wounded.[52]

Lesson

Intelligence reports indicated that the enemy's mission was to destroy the dual bridges (railroad and highway) at the site of the pipe line fire thus cutting a vital link on the only main highway between Qui Nhon and major tactical forces to the north and west. This was probably not a planned ambush. With the arrival of the shuttle convoy, the enemy, for reasons unknown, fired on the column. It has been recommended that the enemy may have mistaken the convoy as a reaction force investigating the pipe line fire. The action by 1LT Stegmayer and his men contributed to the failure of the enemy to accomplish their mission of interdiction of lines of communication to the north and west.

End of the Tet Offensive

The enemy's Tet Offensive had ran its course and turned into a bitter military defeat. The Viet Cong had all but been wiped out and all that was left to fight was the NVA. The NVA retreated back across the border to their sanctuaries to refit, rebuild and plan for their next offensive. The 8th Transportation Group had won the campaign to keep the supply line open. With the end of the Tet Offensive, ambushes on convoys also died down. The NVA would launch a couple more offensives in May and August but with none of the violence of the Tet Offensive. As the enemy took more time to plan, convoy ambushes would become less frequent but in some cases more deadly. The randomness of these ambushes indicated that the enemy only hoped to inflict casualties to wear down American moral and will to continue the war.

12 May 1968

27th and 54th Transportation Battalions

---

[51] Bellino, "8th Transportation."

[52] Bellino, "8th Transportation."

At 1000 hours on 12 May 1968, two convoys approached Bridge 329 (vicinity BR 985856) along Route 1, the coastal highway. The southbound convoy of 17 task vehicles under the control of the 27th Battalion came under M-79 and automatic fire 200 meters south of the Bridge from a squad size enemy force hidden in a tree line 150 to 200 meters on the west side of the road. A northbound convoy of 31 task vehicles plus security, under the control of the 54th Battalion was approaching the same location when the fire began. Both convoys increased speed to clear the 200 meter long kill zone.[53]

The 27th Battalion convoy managed to clear the kill zone with only minor damage to the vehicles but the 54th Battalion convoy suffered one killed in action and the 240th Quartermaster Battalion had one POL tanker driver wounded. The driver of a 2 ½-ton cargo truck was killed and ran off he road onto a small bank. A gun jeep and two gun trucks rendered immediate assistance while directing the convoy through the kill zone. They evacuated the casualties and the convoy continued north without further incident.[54]

The 27th Battalion convoy continued south and reached Bridge 376 (BR 930779) at approximately 1010 hours. There it came under automatic and M-79 fire from a platoon-size enemy force 200 meters from the east side of the road. Upon receiving enemy fire the lead gun truck pulled over and engaged the enemy while the convoy race through the kill zone. Only one driver was wounded and four trucks damaged with bullet holes from both ambushes.[55]

14 August 1968

54th Transportation Battalion

At approximately 1215 hours, 14 August 1968, a convoy under the control of 54th Battalion departed Cha Rang Valley on Route 19 for a line haul trip to Pleiku. The convoy consisted of 68 task vehicles, 7 gun trucks, five gun jeeps armed with M-60 machine guns, and one Quad .50 gun truck.[56]

At 1545 hours, as the first serial of the convoy proceeded west past an area approximately two miles west of Bridge 34, an enemy force dressed in ARVN Marine uniforms attacked the convoy with small arms and B-40 rocket fire. The enemy force was estimated at between a platoon and a company. Four gun trucks, one Quad .50 gun truck and one gun jeep immediately returned fire within the estimated 3,000 meter long kill zone. A reaction force of six APCs and three helicopter gun ships arrived within five minutes after contact. All task vehicles made it out of the kill zone. However, five of those vehicles suffered damage; and one of the five was heavily damaged. The convoy had four men wounded and one soldier from the 1/69th Armored Battalion was killed. The convoy commander reported 12 enemy troops hit by return fire. After the security forces swept the area of contact, they discovered four enemy dead. The five wounded US soldiers were medevaced to the 71st Medical Evacuation Hospital. Of these, two were treated and released.[57]

---

[53] Bellino, "8th Transportation."
[54] Bellino, "8th Transportation."
[55] Bellino, "8th Transportation."
[56] Bellino, "8th Transportation."
[57] Bellino, "8th Transportation."

Lesson

The enemy again varied his tactics by disguising his forces as friendly ARVN troops. Convoy personnel should be suspicious of everything. Be aware of everything familiar and look for clues. While the enemy may be able to dress like friendly soldiers, they make mistakes in dress and behavior.

23 August 1968

88th Transportation Company, 124th Transportation Battalion

The 88th Transportation Company had arrived in Vietnam in August 1966. It was originally a light truck company and was the first truck company that located at Pleiku. It would push cargo out to the smaller camps along the Cambodian border. When the 64th Medium Truck replaced it in May 1967, the 88th had traded in its 5-ton cargo trucks for 12-ton tractors and trailers and became a medium truck company. Its runs usually began with pushing to Pleiku in the morning then going to Qui Nhon in the afternoon to pick up another load. Because it was the only truck company at An Khe, all the trucks in its convoys belonged to its company. For this reason the convoys were generally smaller than those originating from Qui Nhon. When the 124th Battalion arrived in the summer of 1967, the 88th Medium Truck fell under its control.[58]

At 0815 hours on 23 August 1968, a convoy of 30 loaded tractor-trailer combinations under the control of the 88th Transportation Company departed An Khe enroute to Pleiku with 3 gun trucks and 2 gun jeeps in escort. A 2 ½-ton gun truck led the convoy with the convoy commander, LT Mack, riding in the gun jeep which was the third vehicle in the line of march. The second gun truck rode in the middle of the convoy and the last gun truck picked up the rear with the second gun jeep behind it. Only the last gun truck had a radio.[59]

At 0900 hours, an enemy force estimated at two rifle companies attacked the convoy 300 meters west of Check Point 27 just as it was passing by Pump Station #3 at the base of Mang Giang Pass. The enemy fired rockets, mortars and automatic weapons into a kill zone that extended the length of the entire convoy. The lead gun jeep and gun truck raced back into the kill zone while the rear gun truck and gun jeep raced forward to provide cover for the stopped vehicles. Those vehicles that could drove through the kill zone. A mortar round destroyed one tractor-trailer combination and its cargo (Class IV), while six other tractor-trailer combinations were damaged and abandoned in the kill zone. Four others were damaged managed to drive through the kill zone to the top of the Mang Giang Pass where emergency repairs were made and they proceeded on to Pleiku. The rear gun jeep was hit, killing PFC Earl C. Wilson and wounding SGT Capizola and one other passenger. The other three wounded were drivers of task vehicles.[60]

There were three APCs between Bridge 27 and 29 which returned fire. It took 10 to 15 minutes for the reaction force to arrive. Two M42 dusters with twin 40mm cannons were

---

[58] Bellino, "8th Transportation."

[59] Bellino, "8th Transportation."

[60] Bellino, "8th Transportation."

the first reaction force on the scene. No gun ships arrived during the ambush since they were refueling at An Khe. A platoon of APCs which was behind the 88th Transportation Company convoy came up, swept the area and found five enemy dead. Three of the five American wounded were medevaced to An Khe while the other two, who were slightly wounded, continued on with the convoy. The six vehicles abandoned in the kill zone were later policed up by the commander of the 88th Transportation Company in An Khe.[61]

31 August 1968

88th Transportation Company, 124th Transportation Battalion

At 0900 hours on 31 August 1968, a convoy of 33 tractor–trailer combinations under the control of the 88th Transportation Company departed An Khe for Pleiku. Three gun trucks and two gun jeeps escorted the convoy. At 0945 hours, an estimated enemy force of 100 NVA attacked the convoy with mortars, rockets, automatic weapons, small arms and hand grenades between the grid coordinates BR 264468 and BR 256482 below Mang Giang Pass.[62]

There were two APCs in the vicinity of the ambush site and artillery fire was on target in approximately one minute. It took approximately 10 to 15 minutes for a reaction force of five APCs and 6 helicopter gun ships to arrive. The two gunships normally over the column were on the ground in An Khe being refueled. The force was in contact for approximately 30 minutes. They discovered 6 enemy killed.[63]

The convoy had one Soldier killed and six wounded. Four to the six wounded were medevaced to An Khe while the other two with minor wounds continued with the convoy. One gun truck and seven task vehicles became inoperable and were abandoned in the kill zone. Another task vehicle was badly damaged but able to proceed through the kill zone t the top of the Mang Giang Pass to a secure area. The eight vehicles abandoned in the kill zone were recovered by the commanding officer of the 88th TC in An Khe.[64]

Lessons.

The enemy had varied their tactics in terms of what weapons they initiated with, but they usually initiated the ambush with the most lethal weapon whether it was a mine, rocket or mortar to stop the lead vehicle then followed up with small arms and automatic fire to destroy the rest of the trapped vehicles. The ambushes were primarily linear ambushes with forces dug in on both sides of the road. They primarily attacked on the slopes of the mountain passes where vehicles had to slow down. They rarely lasted more than 15 minutes since the arrival of the tanks, APCs and helicopter gun ships tipped the balance of fire power on the side of the Americans.

The enemy began to reduce the length of their kill zones to 200 to 300 meters in length. This reduction and the 100-meter interval between vehicles reduced the number of

[61] Bellino, "8th Transportation."
[62] Bellino, "8th Transportation."
[63] Bellino, "8th Transportation."
[64] Bellino, "8th Transportation."

vehicles in the kill zone and the gun trucks, while in their infancy, bought time for the reaction forces to arrive. Few gun trucks had radios and the convoys still had maintenance vehicles bring up the rear.

1969

359th Transportation Company, 27th Transportation Group

John Dodd was a career soldier and had begun his second tour in Vietnam in December 1968 where he was assigned to the 359th POL Truck Company. The 359th had just transferred from Phu Tai to Pleiku in November 1968 and was attached to the 27th Battalion. It had been attached to the 240th Quartermaster POL Battalion. Once the battalion had connected the pipeline all the way to Pleiku, this discontinued the need for POL trucks to drive Route 19. However, constant pilferage and interdiction by the enemy forced the Quartermaster battalion to shut down the pipeline. From then on POL trucks had to drive to drive the most deadly road in Vietnam. The only load more dangerous than ammunition was hauling 5,000 gallons of jet fuel.[65]

When Dodd arrived, the 359th had only constructed two gun trucks, Brutus and Misfits, and a gun jeep. SGT Prescott helped build and became the first NCOIC of the Brutus, a 5-ton gun truck with two .50s and one 7.62mm mini-gun. Dodd became the NCOIC of the Misfits, a 2 1/2-ton gun truck with an M60 and .50 caliber machinegun in the box. His crew consisted of a driver by the name of Hodges and gunner, Bill Ward. Peter Hish and Alan Wernstrum substituted on the gun truck when any of the crew did not go out.[66]

By this time, 8th Transportation Group had changed its convoy SOP to restrict the size of convoy serials to no more than 30 task vehicles which resulted in two convoy serials leaving with a 20 minute interval between them. The gun truck ration of 1:10 required three gun trucks for a serial of 30 vehicles, but the shortage of gun trucks caused some convoy serials to run with only two. By then all gun trucks had radios so they could communicate with each other and the convoy commanders. This allowed them to operate more independent of the convoy commander. By then all gun trucks had names and seemed to take on personalities as the design of each gun truck was left to the original crews. The crews were all volunteers selected by the old crews from among the best drivers. After COL Garland Ludy would give up command of the 8th Group in October 1969, the crews would paint elaborate art work on the sides of their gun boxes and paint their trucks either dark OD or black.

Gun truck doctrine was for them to enter the kill zone and turn the fight back on the enemy as fast as they could. If any task vehicles were disabled, then the gun trucks would enter the kill zone and protect the vehicles and rescue any wounded or stranded drivers. The gun trucks remained in the companies and more often assigned to platoons so that the élan of the crews did not cause them to lose their identification with the men they protected. The gun truck crews knew at the end of the day, they had to return barracks and face the men they escorted.

---

[65] John Dodd wrote up an account of the 9 June 1969 ambush and brought it to the 2004 Gathering.
[66] Dodd.

9 June 1969

359th Transportation Company, 27th Transportation Battalion

Escorting fuel convoys with each tractor hauling 5,000 gallons of high explosive jet fuel was probably the most dangerous mission for gun trucks. The enemy preferred to hit fuel tankers because the resulting fire usually blocked the road and trapped the other trucks.

On 9 June, the Brutus and Misfits escorted a convoy of 30 fuel tankers out of the Ponderosa to Pleiku. Misfits drove in the middle of the convoy while Brutus brought up the rear. The Brutus was a 5-ton gun truck with two forward left and right M2 .50s and a rear mini-gun. This six-barrel Gatling gun fired 7.62mm rounds at awesome speed, but was prone to misfiring. The mini-gun's rate of fire inspired fear in the enemy. Misfits was a standard 5-ton gun truck with two forward .50s and a dual .50s mounted on a single pedestal in the rear. The convoy had no air support that day. Once they reached An Khe, they would pick up the rest of the tankers from the 359th and the convoy commander, Staff Sergeant Hutcherson.[67]

Just after the convoy had passed the Korean compound at the base of the An Khe Pass, it started received small arms fire. Dodd heard several rounds hit the Misfits' armor plating. At the same time he heard over his radio Specialist 4 Prescott, on Brutus, screaming, "Contact, Contact, Contact!" Dodd saw enemy movement about a hundred yards in the field and returned fire. The gun truck cleared the kill zone and continued up An Khe Pass. Dodd radioed back to Prescott and asked how he was doing. He answered that the Brutus was still involved in fighting and the mini-gun was working. This was unusual as mini-guns were not designed for the road and the bumpy ride tended to knock out the timing mechanism. Prescott had to spend a lot of time working on that mini-gun. When the Misfits reached the top of the Pass, Dodd radioed back to Prescott again to see how the Brutus was holding out. Prescott answered that he had seen abut 30 to 40 enemy and fired the mini-gun on them.[68]

As the road leveled out, the Misfits picked up speed again. It received small arms fire but Dodd did not see anything to shoot at. The excitement passed as they left the danger behind them and the crew of the Misfits returned to their normal "chit chat." They talked mostly about drinking a cold beer when they stopped at An Khe. Dodd joked with the others while he kicked the .50 caliber brass around with his feet. The Misfits had just crossed a bridge about three miles from An Khe. Dodd called in the check point. In a few minutes they would be safe inside the compound.[69]

A few seconds later he heard an explosion behind him. He looked back to see the security force on the bridge was under fire. Dodd recognized the sound of AK47s. This time, Dodd was screaming into the radio, "Contact, Contact, Contact!" He saw VC running around in the field to his left and opened fire with the .50 caliber. Hish and Ward worked as a team firing the M-60 while Wernstrum fired his M-16. Suddenly, someone on the radio asked for their location and size of the enemy force. This struck Dodd odd

---

[67] Dodd.

[68] Dodd.

[69] Dodd.

since he had just called in his location a few seconds before. Right after that a RPG slammed into the front portion of the gun box. The blast from the explosion knocked Dodd's feet out from under him but he did not let go of the machinegun. Wernstrum was bringing up another box of ammunition from the floor for the .50 caliber. Dodd had Hodges pull the gun truck and stop so they could provide fire support until the rest of the tankers past.[70]

The voice on the radio let them know that air support was on the way. Dodd was thinking short bursts with the .50 but his fingers called for long bursts. A second RPG impacted about three feet from the rear of the box. Dodd felt blood hit his eyes. He looked down and saw that he had been hit in the leg, chest and face but with the adrenaline pumping, he felt no pain. As he looked around, he saw that the blast had blown Hish and Wernstrum out of the box. Ward was on the floor clutching his stomach. Dodd realized in a flash that his whole crew was wounded. He then called on the radio that he had two men wounded and needed a medevac.[71]

Hodges climbed up and looked in the gun box. He pointed to some water buffalo where he saw enemy movement. Dodd told him to get back in the cab of the truck and get ready to move out. Dodd picked up another box of ammunition and loaded it. Hish and Wernstrum were still conscious and crawled into the ditch on the side of the road. Pete Hish stood up to climb up on the tail gait when a third RPG hit the rear of the gun box knocking him back to the ground. Dodd saw VC running across the road and fired on the M-60 tank and M-113 APC coming up from the check point. Their fire kept the enemy from overrunning the Misfits. The VC shot Hish twice. Dodd realized that he and Ward were wounded too badly to climb out and rescue the other crew members. Ward needed immediate medical attention. Dodd hit to top of the canvas with his hand and Hodges drove off. Hish then saw the truck pull away and thought, "Oh hell, what am I gonna do now?" He crawled back into the ditch. In half a minute the Misfits had cleared the kill zone. Dodd hoped the medevac would arrive soon. By then Ward was sitting on an ammunition can holding his wound. He had a one inch hole in his stomach. Dodd grabbed a large bandage and told Bill to hold it over the wound.[72]

Dodd then radioed back to Prescott to look for his two missing crew members. Prescott answered that the Brutus had tangled with some NVA after crossing the top of the An Khe Pass. He had already run out of mini-gun ammunition but managed to fight off an enemy rush on his gun truck.[73]

As the truck disappeared, Hish looked up and saw the welcome sight of a medevac helicopter. As the helicopter prepared to land, the pilot and crew saw the enemy dragging wounded off into the jungle.[74]

---

[70] Dodd.
[71] Dodd.
[72] Dodd.
[73] Dodd.
[74] Dodd.

The Misfits pulled into An Khe where the trucks had assembled. Hodges stopped the gun truck but Dodd told him to drive straight to the field hospital. As the gun truck drove thirty miles per hour though the gate of Camp Radcliffe, the MPs saw that they were in trouble. Two MPs jumped in a jeep and led them to the hospital. Dodd was looking after Ward when he saw that Hodges had the front bumper trailing just about two inches behind the lead jeep. The MP looked back at Dodd and the NCOIC motioned for the MPs to speed up or get run over.[75]

Once at the hospital, the medics helped the two wounded soldiers from the gun truck and put them onto tables in the receiving area. The medics rushed Bill Ward straight to the Xray. The medics cut Dodd's clothes off and the doctor began pulling pieces of metal out of his legs. He informed Dodd that the blood on his face came from the missing tip of his nose. Dodd's real concern was further down his anatomy. Hr kept trying to lift himself up to see what the doctor was doing to his legs. The nurse kept pushing him back down. Because Dodd persisted in trying to rise up, she took her hands from his chest then grabbed his "family jewels" and told him not to worry, everything was okay. Dodd laid back and relaxed.[76]

While the doctors worked on Dodd, the medics brought in a wounded VC and put him on the table next to him. In a loud voice, Dodd told asked them to move that SOB away a few more feet from Dodd. Another nurse came in and told Dodd that his two missing crew members had been brought in. Pete Hish had fragmentary wounds and was shot twice. Alan Wernstrum also suffered from fragmentary wounds and lost part of his hand. The four wounded crew members had a short reunion in the medical ward. Because of the seriousness of the other three's wounds, they were medevaced to Japan that evening. Since the hospital at An Khe had become crowded, Dodd was flown to Pleiku. From there, he hitchhiked rides to his company area. He did light work supervising the local help around the company for about 30 days until his wounds healed then he rode on South Vietnamese convoys calling in check points until he left Vietnam in October 1969.[77]

Lesson

The enemy employed two kill zones, the first most likely to draw off the gun trucks so that the next ambush would catch the convoy of fuel tankers unprotected. Probably one of the boldest moves the enemy had made yet, in their effort at unpredictability, they had launched the main ambush right outside the compound at An Khe where most drivers felt relatively safe.

Radios in each of the gun trucks made them more responsive to enemy action and allowed them to act independent of the convoy commander. However, this placed greater decision making responsibility on the crews of the gun trucks.

---

[75] Dodd.

[76] Dodd.

[77] Dodd.

Misfits' gun box took three hits from RPGs, yet one gunner still continued to put up a fight. The gun trucks would take great punishment and still continue to fight due to the dedication of the crews. By then all the gun trucks had names and began to take on personalities. Each had its own design and different arrangement of weapons systems. From then on, ambushes would be described in terms of the gun trucks as if they were living things.

4 January 1970

54th Transportation Battalion

A convoy left the marshalling yard at Cha Rang Valley one morning of 4 January 1970 bound for An Khe and Pleiku along Route 19. The convoy was divided into serials of no more than 30 vehicles with two gun trucks and one gun jeep as escort. The serials kicked out at 20 minute intervals. Most ambushes took place in either of the two passes, An Khe or Mang Giang. Drivers felt rather safe in the coastal plane since the Republic of Korea (ROK) Tiger Division secured the area. All the ROKs had lived through the Korean War and hated communists. They also felt extremely proud to have the opportunity to serve in Vietnam. They were disciplined soldiers but extremely brutal in their pursuit of the enemy.[78]

The lead serial was caught in an ambush at Hogson village between two bridges below An Khe Pass. A couple hundred yards away on the south side of the road (left) was a small ridge surmounted with a Buddhist temple. The ridge dropped off into a rice paddy that stretched north of the road. The lead convoy called for support.[79]

SGT Roger D. Champ, platoon sergeant of 1st Platoon 523rd Light Truck, rode in the Eve of Destruction in the following serial. The Eve was a 5-ton gun truck with two forward left and right .50s and dual mounted .50s on a single pedestal in the rear. Uncle Meat brought up the rear. Uncle Meat was also a standard 5-ton gun truck but with three .50s, two forward and one rear.

Upon receiving the call for help the Eve and Uncle Meat raced full throttle up to the kill zone. By the time they arrived the fight had gone on for half an hour or more. Several task vehicles, both gun trucks and the gun jeep were shot up. The two new gun trucks maneuvered around the disabled vehicles. Mortar and rocket fire fell like rain drops but fell short in rice paddy. This was the worst ambush that SGT Champ had ever seen. As soon as he reached the kill zone, he called in helicopter gun ships from An Khe, but they reported that they were "socked in" by weather. Champs saw no cloud in the sky.[80]

The Eve nosed itself into position at a 45 degree angle in the kill zone and stopped behind a disabled vehicle. This allowed all machineguns to fire forward. SGT Champ saw puffs of smoke in the temple and fired at it. A 2 ½-ton truck from the 4th Infantry Division (Mechanized), which had infiltrated the convoy, tried to run the kill zone. As it

[78] Roger D. Champ interview by Richard Killblane, 18 June 2005.
[79] Champ interview.
[80] Champ interview, 18 June 2005 and telephone interview 1 September 2005.

maneuvered around the Eve off the road on the north side, a B40 rocket disabled it wounding the driver. The gunners fired continuously.[81]

They had been in the kill zone for about an hour when a mortar round hit near the edge of Champ's gun truck and shrapnel blew a gunner out of the gun box onto the pavement between the gun truck and disabled truck in front of them. Champ jumped down to rescue him. The sergeant examined the gunner's wounds. The gunner had worn his flak vest open and received a sucking chest wound. As Champ bent over to administer first aid, pieces of asphalt began hitting him in his face. For the first time he realized that they were also receiving small arms fire. When he looked up he assumed that the only place the small arms fire could come from was the banana grove that ran along the irrigation ditch a couple hundred yards away. Champ then drug the wounded gunner around to safety behind the truck. He also dragged a wounded Vietnamese man who unfortunately was caught in the kill zone. He then climbed back into the gun box and directed the other gunners to fire into the banana grove. Suddenly enemy soldiers rose up and began running away. To their shock, the Koreans had secretly positioned themselves behind the enemy and cut them down. This broke the enemy attack. According to his award citation the ambush had lasted three hours.[82]

A Huey gun ship finally arrived at 1000 hours after the fighting died down. He had put in a call for a medevac but none would respond. He then called down the Huey gun ship and loaded the wounded gunner, a Vietnamese man, and the wounded 4th ID soldier in the Huey. The infantry driver told Champ that he had just reenlisted. All the tires of the Eve were shot out. A tire truck came up and the crew of the Eve replaced the tires. Any trucks that could not be repaired on the road were hooked up to a bob tail and towed.[83]

The next day when the convoy rode past the same area, the Koreans had stacked all the enemy dead alongside the road to show the truck drivers. This was common practice for the Koreans. They were proud and liked to show the Americans their kills before they burned them. There were so many dead that it took a truck load of fuel to burn them.[84]

Lessons

The enemy had taken advantage of two situations, the inability of the helicopters to fly and attacking in an area where the drivers relaxed their guard. The availability of air support and response time of the local combat arms usually limited most ambushes to no more than 15 minutes. The absence of these caused the enemy to fight longer.

Since the enemy reduced the size of the kill zones they tended to let the lead trucks pass and attack the middle or rear of the convoy. The organization of the convoy into serials of 20 to 30 vehicles kept at least two gun trucks within supporting distance. The arrival of the two additional gun trucks turned the fight back on the enemy. Roger Champ felt that the combined machineguns of his two gun trucks were enough to beat back the

---

[81] Champ telephone interview.
[82] Champ interview 18 June 2005 and telephone interview 1 September 2005.
[83] Champ interview 18 June 2005 and telephone interview 1 September 2005.
[84] Champ interview 18 June 2005 and telephone interview 1 September 2005.

enemy ambush. It was a question of superior and accurate fire that won the day. The Korean soldiers that were maneuvering to flank the enemy were in position prevented the enemy from escaping. For his actions, SGT Champ was awarded the Silver Star Medal.[85]

1 April 1970

54th Transportation Battalion

On 1 April 1970, two westbound convoy serials headed up towards An Khe Pass. The Iron Butterfly was the rear gun truck of the first serial. The Matchbox was the middle gun truck in the second serial and Uncle Meat brought up the rear. The convoy commander ran up and down the convoy serial in his gun jeep. All were standard 5-ton gun trucks but Iron Butterfly had four corner mounted .50s instead of just the usual three.[86]

Just short of the Hairpin at An Khe Pass, an RPG hit the Iron Butterfly right in the hood and disabled it. Four to five 5-ton cargo trucks were shot up but only one driver was wounded. The vehicles that could drove through the kill zone to camp at An Khe under the escort of the lead gun truck. Iron Butterfly drove into ditch and remained in the kill zone and put up a fight.

The Matchbox, in the following serial, drove up to assist the trucks left in the kill zone. Someone made the decision for the trucks behind the kill zone to turn around and head back down to Cha Rang Valley. When some of the 5-tons towing 105 howitzers turned around they backed the tubes into the side of the mountain causing them to flip upside down. The Matchbox had a hard time dodging the trucks and bouncing 105s to get up to the kill zone. When it did the crew of the Matchbox asked the crew of the disabled Iron Butterfly if they wanted to leave their truck. They did not want to leave so the Matchbox gave them some .50 ammunition and proceeded on up around the Hairpin. The Iron Butterfly had fired off almost all its ammunition. They received some mortar rounds and small arms fire. Probably four to six cargo trucks were disabled, but the only one driver was injured. The Matchbox took him to the top of the Pass for a medevac then returned to clean up the ambush site.

Uncle Meat came up with some reactionary forces walking in behind it. Uncle Meat gave the Iron Butterfly a push and it started. The Iron Butterfly drove up the pass on its own power. Surprisingly, Koreans soldiers came out of the ditch where the ambush had been and used the Uncle Meat for cover and followed it up the Pass.

Lesson

The enemy had initiated the ambush with an RPG on the gun truck in the rear of the convoy following by small arms and automatic fire. They had selected the Hairpin where the traffic had to slow down to 4 mph and had trouble not bunching up.

An ambush is a planned attack with the element of surprise. This element of surprise allows the enemy to select the first vehicle to destroy. Once the ambush has been sprung,

[85] Champ telephone interview.

[86] Larry Fiandt interview, 14 Sep 05.

then it becomes a contest of firepower. The NVA soon learned to take out the gun truck first. Dividing convoys into serials of 20 to 30 vehicles driving within supporting distance proved to be a wise decision. This allowed two to three gun trucks from the next serial to reinforce the gun truck in the kill zone.

10 June 1970

27th Transportation Battalion

At 0845 hours on 10 June 1970, a 17 vehicle westbound convoy reached the Hairpin just below the An Khe Pass and traffic slowed to a crawl. A refrigeration van at the head of the convoy was traveling about three to five miles per hour when an NVA soldier stood up on a slight rise to the south side of the road and opened fire with his AK47 at approximately 25 meters. He seriously damaged the engine of the tractor and shot out several tires. The driver continued to drive for about 100 meters when another enemy soldier fired a B40 rocket into the rear of his van. The convoy then came under enemy fire from both sides of the road. The tractor pulling the reefer continued driving and managed to clear his vehicle out of the kill zone. Meanwhile, the enemy opened fire with small arms and automatic weapons from base of the Hairpin curve to approximately 400 meters east of it and disabled a 40-foot Low Boy, of the 444th Medium Truck Company, that was following directly behind the reefer van.[87]

PFC Billy Wehunt, of the 444th Medium Truck Company, drove his 5-ton tractor into the kill zone in an attempt to clear the area of US personnel. As he approached the Low Boy, the enemy fired into his cab killing him and the tractor drove off the side of the road. The convoy commander was with the lead element of the convoy at the base of the Hairpin Curve. Upon hearing the initial firing, he organized those vehicles ahead of the 200 meter kill zone and led them to the top of the Pass. At the same time, a 444th gun truck drove into the kill zone to recover PFC Wehunt from his vehicle, but came under intense small arms fire. Two MP V-100 armored cars arrived and the gun truck crew tried again to recover the body of their fellow driver, but intense enemy fire again forced them back. Finally, two more gun trucks from the following convoy arrived and the combined fire power of five gun platforms provided enough covering fire for the recovery of PFC Wehunt's body. The enemy broke contact at 0945 hours, an hour after the ambush had started. The gun trucks checked all areas of the kill zone for more personnel then proceeded to the top of the Pass. The Americans had lost one man killed, four wounded with three vehicles damaged.[88]

Lesson

This time the ambush was sporadic at the start as if it was not well planned or rehearsed, however, the intensity of the fire was enough to drive back several gun trucks. The enemy used the similar tactic and location as the 1 April Ambush.

It took the combined fire power of three gun trucks and two V-100 armored cars to turn the fight back on the enemy.

---

[87]COL David H. Thomas, "Vehicle Convoy Security Operations in the Republic of Vietnam," Active Project No. ACG-78F, US Army Contact Team in Vietnam, APO San Francisco, CA 96384, 30 Sep 71.

[88] Thomas, "Convoy Security Operations."

15 June 1970

27th Transportation Battalion

"At approximately 0900, 15 June 1970, a convoy under the control of the 27th Battalion traveling up the An Khe Pass encountered an enemy mortars or rockets. The ambush I referred to happened on 15 Jun 1970 at the hairpin turn in the An Khe Pass. As usually happens when things go bad everything goes wrong. My radio hadn't been working all morning. I never received any answers to my check point call-ins. My driver that day, a great buck sergeant, named Calvin Wood, and I had just passed up through the convoy and got the drivers to open up their interval. We dropped back in at the rear of the convoy about 200 meters below the hairpin turn when mortars or rockets started hitting above the turn. I called contact on the radio and Sgt Wood immediately headed for the kill zone.[89]

"When we rounded the hairpin, I had one tractor trailer stopped in the road and another truck was passing him. The King Cobra was ahead of the kill zone when the ambush started but backed down into the kill zone and was laying down fire. Sgt Wood drove between the stopped truck and the one passing and as he did the driver of the truck passing was hit and went in the ditch up against the embankment. We drove up and turned around and came back to the hairpin. The trail gun truck came into the kill zone to help, then Sgt Wood and I went to check the drivers of the stopped trucks. The remaining trucks had driven through and out of the kill zone. The driver of the first stopped truck was initially missing, but I later found out that when his truck was disabled by a rocket and he was wounded by shrapnel he had jumped on one of the other trucks driving through. We got the other driver out of the truck in the ditch and took him to the top of the pass where a Huey that just happened to be flying by landed and we put him on it and they took him to An Khe. Unfortunately he died. Four rounds of automatic fire had hit the cab of his truck, three were stopped by the armor plate in the door but one had come through the canvas top and hit him. While all this was going on the gun trucks and jeeps from a convoy we had passed at the bottom of the pass had come up to help us. I used one of their gun jeep radios to talk to Battalion for the first time. We then made another pass through the ambush site to get the gun trucks to brake contact. At the top of the pass we got some additional fire from the VC but suffered no more damage.[90]

"We then headed for An Khe. At the next bridge we found one of my reefers. The van had been hit by a rocket and the cab by 11 automatic rounds. The driver had been wounded in the leg but, had driven to the top of the pass where a shot gunner, riding in an engineer low boy that had tagged alone with our convoy, got out and drove my guy's rig up to the bridge. The Infantry guys at the bridge were tending to my wounded driver and had called in a medevac for him. My lead NCO had crossed over the top of the pass and had switched his radio to the next security net before the ambush started and didn't know anything had happened. They had to send gun trucks out of An Khe to chase the front half of the convoy down and bring them back to An Khe. We spent a couple hours getting reorganized and taking care of things regarding the wounded (found out the missing driver was at the hospital with minor shrapnel wounds) and the KIA then went on to

---

[89] LTC (R) Ronald Voightritter email to Richard Killblane.

[90] Voightritter email.

Pleiku. We later took some mortar rounds in the Mang Giang Pass but, they didn't hit anything and we kept moving on. We didn't get to Pleiku until about 1500 so we RON'd there and came back to Phu Tai the next morning. I can tell you the use of gun trucks and the armor plating of drivers doors was a major life savor for 8th Group truckers. This was my first contact in 9 months being in country. I had a few more but, nothing like this one, thank goodness."[91]

Two vehicles were damaged with one soldier killed and three wounded in the ambush that lasted 35 minutes. It took place 100 meters west from where the last ambush occurred five days earlier. CPT Voightritter received the Silver Star medal for his actions and SGT Calvin Woods was awarded the Bronze Star Medal with V device.

Lesson

The last three ambushes were in the vicinity of the Hairpin. The last two were within days of each other. The enemy seemed to deliberately want to confuse the Americans to any pattern since ambushes had become less frequent. The object of their new tactics was to get the convoys to drop their guard either by selecting locations where the convoys felt safe or changing the frequency of the ambushes.

The convoy interval had reduced the number of vehicles in the kill zone, so the enemy could only expect to damage or destroy a few vehicles at best. The enemy usually ambushed the middle or rear of the lead convoy. This split the convoy. The lead element automatically continued to safety with one gun truck as escort. That way, they only had to contend with the rear gun truck, before the others from the next convoy could arrive.

If the convoy commander was at the head of his convoy when the ambush split it, he was not in a position where the decisions needed to be made. The rear of the convoy increasingly became the location where critical decisions had to be made. The employment of convoy serials proved over and again the best method for mutual support. The gun trucks of the next serial could always seem to respond quicker than any combat arms reaction force.

21 November 1970

27th Transportation Battalion

By 1970, the 359th Medium Petroleum Truck Company had the gun trucks Misfits, Brutus, Outlaws, Woom Doom and Ball of Confusion. The crew of Brutus consisted of William "Bill" Kagel, Ernest "Ernie" Quintana, and Sergeant Jimmy Ray Callison. The Brutus was a 5-ton gun truck with two forward left and right M2 .50s and a rear mini-gun. On the morning of 21 November 1970, a jeep with radio led the 27th Battalion convoy serial of 29 vehicles headed toward Pleiku. Brutus followed 16th in the line of march and the maintenance gun truck, Ball of Confusion, followed in the rear. Ball of Confusion was one of the old 2 ½-ton gun trucks armed with two M60s. Behind it followed a gun jeep with the convoy commander, an NCO from the 359th Medium Truck. A newly assigned lieutenant rode along in the jeep as an observer to gain experience. Having just passed an eastbound 27th Battalion convoy, the convoy with Brutus began

[91] Voightritter email.

climbing up toward Mang Giang Pass. The south side of the road sloped upward and the north side sloped downward. Tall grass and scattered thickets bordered both sides of the road with the tree line 250 meters from the road.[92]

At 1105 hours, the middle of the convoy came under rocket, automatic and small-arms fire from the south side of the road. The 800 meter kill zone caught Brutus and six fuel tankers. The crew of Brutus called "Contact, Contact, Contact" over the radio and immediately returned fire with a .50 caliber and mini-gun. B40 rockets ignited two of the tankers and another jack knifed partially blocking the road. Small-arms fire punctured the tanks and flattened the tires on the three other tankers but they drove out of the kill zone, picked up the drivers of the burning tankers while leaking a trail of fuel on the road. The Brutus joined the lead vehicles at the top of the pass and halted. The vehicles behind Brutus halted, turned around and drove back down the road. Ball of Confusion and the convoy commander's jeep were two miles back down the road assisting a broken down vehicle. For the first few minutes of the ambush, Brutus bore the brunt of the fight.[93]

Upon hearing "Contact," the convoy commander and three gun trucks of the 597th Medium Truck in the eastbound convoy; Sir Charles, King Cobra, and Poison Ivy, turned around and raced to the kill zone. Sir Charles was an APC gun truck with a forward .50 mounted on the TC hatch and two left and right rear M60s on the troop hatch. King Cobra was also an APC gun truck but had three .50s. Poison Ivy was a standard 5-ton gun truck. Ball of Confusion had preceded them. Because the jack-knifed tanker blocked the road, the gun trucks bunched up on the east end of the kill zone and placed suppressive fire with all their weapons into the enemy position. A rocket hit the gun box on Brutus, wounding Kagel and Quintana and killing Callison. The Ball of Confusion also had one man wounded in the fighting.[94]

This ambush was timed with an enemy attack on Landing Zone Attack, just three miles down the road. Within 15 minutes of the first call, six APCs and one tank of the 1st Battalion, 10th ARVN Cavalry arrived in the kill zone. The majority of the ARVN Cavalry Squadron, which had responsibility for this area, had been pulled up to Pleiku several days before for operations in that area. After another 5 minutes of fighting, the enemy withdrew and only sporadic firing continued for another 15 minutes when two gun ships arrived.[95]

Ronald "Ron" Mallory, Richard Bond and Chuck Hauser had previously become friends with the crew of the Brutus. Every time the "Brutus" returned from a convoy, Mallory and his friends liked to help take the weapons off and clean them. They were curious and wanted to know everything about the gun truck. One day the crew told their friends, "If anything ever happens to us, we'd like you all to take over the gun truck." In that manner the crew of the Brutus had chosen their replacements. Ron Mallory, Chuck Hauser,

[92] Ronald Mallory interview by Richard Killblane, 14 June 2004 and Thomas, "Vehicle Convoy Security," p. B-1-4.
[93] Thomas, "Vehicle Convoy Security," p. B-1-4.
[94] Thomas, "Vehicle Convoy Security," p. B-1-4, Mallory and Freeman interviews.
[95] Thomas, "Vehicle Convoy Security," p. B-1-4.

Larry Dahl and Sergeant Richard Bond replaced the crew of Brutus. Because Mallory was one of the best drivers at split shifting, he naturally became the driver. Sergeant Bond assumed the responsibility as the NCOIC with Hauser and Dahl the gunners. As the new crew set about cleaning and repairing the gun truck, the loss of their friends saddened them. To give the truck a new look, they completely repainted Brutus. They thought this would make the old crew proud of what they had done. It took about a week to put Brutus back on the road, but took almost a month for the smell of blood to leave.[96]

SP5 Erik Freeman replaced the wounded man on Ball of Confusion and became the NCOIC. He had reenlisted for a second tour in Vietnam just to be an NCOIC of a gun truck in 8th Group. The rest of the crew was due to rotate home so he ended up picking a whole new crew and rebuilding the gun truck. Freeman replaced the 2 ½-ton with a 5-ton cargo truck and replaced the two M60s with forward and rear mounted M2 .50 caliber machineguns and left and right mini-guns. Freeman manned the mini-guns while the other two gunners manned the .50s. He named his new gun truck, The Untouchable.[97]

Lesson

It is possible that the enemy had hoped the attack on the landing zone would have drawn off the reaction force, however, the gun trucks held their own in this fight and the reaction force arrived. The gun trucks with their wild names and fancy artwork had added to the élan of the gun truck crews. This élan made them more independent of command and caused them to react without hesitation. The crews knew that the key to turning the fight back on the enemy was to mass greater fire power against the enemy. As soon as the call, "contact," went out, all available gun trucks would rush into the kill zone.

16 December 1970

54th Transportation Battalion

On 16 December 1970, in a westbound convoy, Satan's Chariot passed a broken-down tractor and trailer and two gun trucks from an earlier convoy at An Khe Pass. Satan's Chariot was a 5-ton gun truck with three .50s, one forward and two rear. The convoy arrived at the 54th Transportation Battalion base camp just an hour before dark. Sergeant Charles Sims, the NCOIC of Satan's Chariot, had his men take off the weapons and start cleaning them when the commander of the 88th Light Truck arrived and told him to have his gun truck escort a spare tractor back up to retrieve the disabled vehicle. Sims challenged the decision. At that hour they would reach the pass after dark. Nothing traveled on the roads at night. He felt the gun truck should just pick up the driver, abandon the truck, and return. The battalion commander gave Sims a direct order to recover the vehicle. The commander knew that if the tractor was left unattended over night the Explosive Ordinance Demolitions men would have to clear the vehicle the next day before a convoy could pass. Any vehicle left unattended on the road was automatically considered mined. This would delay the departure of the convoys by an hour. Sims departed with a spare tractor and wrecker to transfer the trailer.[98]

---

[96] Ronald Mallory interview by Richard Killblane, 14 June 2004.

[97] Erik Freeman interview by Richard Killblane, 11 July 2002.

[98] Email correspondence between Erik Freeman and Charles Sims, 15 – 21 February 1998.

When they arrived, Sims saw that the MP V-100 armored car that closed down the road each night was providing security for the broken-down tractor. Sir Charles also arrived. Once they recovered the tractor and trailer, Satan's Chariot led the way followed by the wrecker towing the tractor and trailer, Sir Charles then the armored car. When they reached the base of the mountain, they found that the Koreans had strung a concertina barricade across the road closing Bridge Number 8. Sims radioed their situation to the road controller. The controller, in turn, called the American liaison officer with the Koreans to have them open the bridges. After waiting 20 minutes, the Koreans received instructions to open the bridge.[99]

Sims had driven the road so many times he thought he could have done it blindfolded, but it did not look the same in the dark. He did not remember the small village located on the north side of the road near the next bridge. Since there were no lights, he did not have visual cues to remind him of its location. To Sims surprise, the next bridge was also closed. These delays made them a target for a hasty ambush. They waited for another 10 minutes for the Koreans to open the barricades. They slowly negotiated around the barricades and all but the last gun truck and armored car had crossed the bridge when an explosion hit Sir Charles. The convoy started receiving small-arms fire from the village on the north side of the road. Somebody screamed over the radio, "Contact!" The gun trucks, the armored car, and the Koreans immediately returned fire.

The maintenance gun truck, The Untouchable, had just towed a vehicle back to Cha Rang Valley. On his return, Freeman became concerned that two trucks up on An Khe Pass might have to remain there over night. He had a policy that he would never leave any of the vehicles or drivers behind if at all possible. On his way back to camp, Freeman passed Satan's Chariot and the wrecker heading back up to the Pass.[100]

Upon dropping off the tractor, Freeman's crew changed a flat and refueled while he monitored the radio. He could hear they were having trouble hooking up the broken-down tractor and worried that the Koreans would close the bridges on them when it became dark. Fearing that his commanding officer would not let him back out on the road at night, Freeman and his crew loaded up in The Untouchable and left without permission. According to policy, MPs at the gate were not allowed to stop a gun truck. Fortunately The Untouchable found all the bridges open except Bridge Number 7. The Koreans let The Untouchable onto the bridge but would not let it cross. When Freeman saw the recovery convoy approaching, he convinced the Koreans to let his truck drive off the west end of the bridge to turn around. The Untouchable backed up and turned around then pulled up alongside the bridge so it would be ready to fall in with the convoy when it passed. Just as the wrecker crossed the bridge, The Untouchable pulled into the convoy. Small-arms fire broke out from the village lasting about a minute. The rocket blast had mortally wounded the NCOIC of Sir Charles in the head.[101]

---

[99] Ibid.

[100] Freeman-Sims email and Freeman interview.

[101] Freeman interview.

When the ambush started, the Koreans quickly closed all the bridge barricades. Freeman had just told his driver to back up when he heard the ambush, but The Untouchable was trapped on the bridge with Sir Charles and the armored car behind the bridge. Satan's Chariot could not reenter the bridge, so Sims led the wrecker back to Cha Rang. The rest of the bridges were open and he received a flare ship to escort his convoy back. Meanwhile, one of the gunners on The Untouchable pointed his .50 caliber machinegun at the Koreans, forcing them to open the bridge's west end. The Untouchable then turned around and pulled up next to Sir Charles. Freeman then raked the tree line with the mini gun for about 10 to 15 seconds and the other vehicles got under way and crossed the bridge. A medevac picked up the NCOIC, but he was already dead. An attack helicopter and flare ship escorted Freeman's convoy back. This verified that any prolonged halt made vehicles a target of opportunity since local VC lived in the area.[102]

A local Vietnamese who lived in the village was killed in cross fire. The next day, the Vietnamese had painted a message on the road claiming that the Americans had killed her. This became an international incident, but the chain of command backed their gun truck crews.

Lesson

This was a hasty ambush by a small enemy force that took advantage of the delay in recovering the broken down tractor. The enemy also liked to fire on the Americans from villages so that some of them might be killed by the return fire. They could use this as part of their propaganda.

Well intended plans resulted in a series of delays in recovery and for whatever reason; there was a serious break down in coordination with the Koreans on opening the bridges after dark. Murphy's Law trapped these vehicles out on Route 19 after dark, a dangerous place to be. In spite of these mistakes, the dedication of the gun truck crews to not leave anyone behind brought several gun trucks to the aid of one disabled tractor and trailer. In an ambush, the side with the superior fire power usually wins.

23 February 1971

27th Transportation Battalion

On 23 February 1971, SGT Bond had the day off so SGT Hector Diaz filled in as the NCOIC of the Brutus that day. Although SPC4 Chuck Huser was not the NCOIC, he operated the radio since he knew the truck. The driver of the Playboys went on sick call so the NCOIC SGT Grailin Weeks, asked Walter Deeks to fill in for him. Playboys was a gun truck in the 545th Light Truck but was a spare that day and was asked to escort fuel tankers of the 359th POL. Walter did not like escorting tankers because they tend to explode when hit by rockets, but he could not turn down a request. Gun truck crews were considered the elite of truck drivers. They did not turn down missions and many drove right up to the day they had to leave for the United States.[103]

---

[102] Freeman-Sims email and Freeman interview.
[103] Freeman, Deeks, and Mallory interviews.

That day, a convoy under the control of the 27th returning from Pleiku ran into an ambush at the top of An Khe Pass. NVA company of about 50 initiated the ambush by disabling the gun truck, Creeper, with a rocket that blew out the tires. SGT McCatchin, NCOIC of the Creeper, called for help. The Playboys immediately responded to the call of contact and raced into the kill zone. One NVA soldier stood up in the ditch near the hill to fire his B40 rocket at the cab of the Playboys. Walter Deeks stopped the gun truck so the rocket passed overhead, while the crew killed the enemy soldier with the .50 machine gun. The Playboys then proceeded around the bend into the kill zone. One 5,000-gallon fuel tanker had been hit and was leaking fuel on the road and another had jack-knifed in the road. The driver had abandoned it. They saw that the immobilized Creeper still placed suppressive fire on the enemy.[104]

The convoy commander, a lieutenant, rode in the Playboys. He directed that the gun truck pull right up next to the disabled fuel truck about thirty yards from the Creeper. The Playboys placed suppressive fire on the enemy and Deeks saw about 15 enemy soldiers either running away from the fire or moving to a better cover. The fighting continued for nearly twenty minutes, which seemed like an eternity to those in it. The convoy commander called for air support and a tank to come up from the nearest check point and help. Whenever there would be a lull in the fighting, more enemy soldiers would move to a better position and the fighting would intensify again.[105]

The gun trucks of the 359th Transportation Company, Misfits, Brutus and The Untouchable, asked if they needed help and joined from the following convoy serial. The Brutus had stopped near the embankment where the NVA soldier had fired the B40 rocket at the Playboys. The ambush then had five gun trucks and a tank firing on the enemy. During the fighting, the mini-gun on the Brutus jammed and Hector Diaz and Chuck Huser quickly went to work to get it back in action. An NVA soldier stood up and lobbed a grenade into the Brutus. Without hesitation, Larry Dahl jumped on the grenade saving the lives of his crew members. The other crews saw the explosion in the box and knew the crew was seriously hurt. Ron Mallory heard the explosion then was covered with blood.[106]

The crews of the gun trucks had developed a special bond of friendship. Many gun truck members expressed the same opinion that any crew member would have done the same thing to save the lives of their crew. Larry just saw the grenade first. Wounded but conscious, Huser called for Ron Mallory over the internal radio to get out of there. Ron Mallory then maneuvered the truck out of the kill zone and raced his gun truck to the next friendly check point where a medevac awaited for the wounded crew members.[107]

Meanwhile the enemy fire died down again so the lieutenant told Deeks to get out and look for the driver of the disabled truck. He wanted to rescue the drivers and get out of the kill zone. For some reason Deeks ran around to the far side door. As he rounded the

---

[104] Deeks interview.
[105] Ibid.
[106] Freeman, Deeks, and Mallory interviews.
[107] Mallory interview.

front of the truck, he saw a young, scared NVA soldier staring up at him from under the wheel well. The kid did not look older than 14 years of age. Deeks had not taken his M-16 with him. He then spun around and ran back the way he came. He shouted to the gunners, "There's one under that truck, there's one under that truck." Loudon yelled, "There he goes." He then shot and killed the enemy soldier.[108]

Someone yelled that they saw the driver behind the truck. The blast had blown him out of the truck. Deeks was tall and had played basketball in high school. He ran over and picked the wounded driver up in his arms. The unconscious driver was peppered with shrapnel. He carried him over to the gun truck and the crew threw down the first aid kit. He patched the worst wounds while the crew called for a medevac. The helicopter landed and Deeks carried the driver to it. He felt very vulnerable to enemy fire. Deeks covered in the driver's blood returned to the cab of his gun truck.[109]

The lieutenant then asked if anyone knew how to drive a tanker. He wanted the jack-knifed tanker moved out of the kill zone. At great risk to himself, Grailin Weeks climbed in the tractor with its 5,000-gallon fuel tank behind it then turned it around and drove it out of the kill zone. The gun trucks followed. The enemy had been dug in and seemed to have been determined to destroy the trucks. The ambush had lasted for nearly one hour, a lot longer than the usual 10 to 15 minutes. The convoy passed the infantry on their way to mop up the ambush site.[110]

The convoy stopped at the check point and the lieutenant told Deeks to get a count of trucks and drivers. He was still shaking from the ambush. Once out of harms way, they could relax a little. The shock of the event finally caught up with Deeks. As he was trying to get a count he fell on his knees and started vomiting. The other drivers got the head count for him. Meanwhile Weeks began to go shake uncontrollably and went into spasms. The convoy commander called for a medevac to take him back to the hospital where he could calm down.[111]

Grailin Weeks received the Silver Star Medal and the rest of the crew of the Playboys earned Bronze stars with V device. Larry Dahl was posthumously awarded the Medal of Honor. A new crew took over the Brutus. Dahl's Medal of Honor proved that even truck drivers could be heroes too.

The loss of his friends caused, Ron Mallory to quit driving and he worked in the motor pool until he rotated back to the United States. Hector went through extensive medical treatment and died in 2003 of Hepatitis, which he picked up in a blood transfusion. Huser returned from the hospital to join the crew of the Misfits.[112]

Lessons

[108] Deeks interview.
[109] Ibid.
[110] Ibid.
[111] Ibid.
[112] Deeks interview.

One of the obvious conclusions was that the enemy felt very brave with the absence of air cover. The enemy continued to initiate ambushes by attacking the gun trucks first. The enemy was either determined to destroy the remaining trucks in the kill zone or the quick arrival of the Playboys prevented them from escaping. The crew could not determine if the enemy was maneuvering to attack or escape.

The arrival of the three additional gun trucks from the next serial turned the tide of the battle. Against a determined enemy, it took as many as five gun trucks with three to four machineguns each to beat back their assault. Even then, this was just enough to defend the disabled vehicles and rescue drivers. It took the arrival of the security force flanked the enemy.

Action Taken

After that ambush, 7th Squadron, 17th Air Cavalry was required to low and slow over the convoys. At first they flew around the country side but that did not deter the enemy from ambushing the convoys. The helicopters were directed to fly low and slow along the roads looking for wires and enemy spider holes. They flew so low that the drivers could reach up and touch the skids. This was boring duty for the pilots but they challenged their flying skills by landing on the back of moving trailers or following between the trucks in the convoy.[113]

16 March 1971

359th Transportation Company

On 16 March 1971, the 512th Transportation Company was ambushed west of An Khe village. Four vehicles were disabled by enemy fire. The company had no maintenance capability with it and was forced to abandon the trucks where they were hit. Within 5 minutes, the maintenance gun truck, The Untouchable, came to their rescue. Within three hours of work by the crew, they had repaired or recovered all damaged vehicles and towed them to a secure perimeter.[114]

2. I Tactical Zone

In December 1967, MACV sent truck companies under the control of the 57th Transportation Battalion north into I Corps Tactical Zone to support the recent movement of the 1st Cavalry Division in that area. Shortly thereafter, the number of truck companies required a second truck battalion, the 39th. The 57th Battalion would support US Army units in the southern part of the Zone and the 39th Battalion would support the US Army units in the northern half of the Zone. Since some of the companies came out of the 8th Group, they brought their gun trucks and SOPs with them. Therefore the convoy doctrine and tactics closely resembled those of the 8th Group.

12 April 1968

---

[113] Paul Blosser interview by Richard Killblane, 9 June 2002 and LTC Alvin C. Ellis, "Operational Report – Lessons Learned, 39th Transportation Battalion (Truck), Period Ending 30 April 1971, RCS CSFOR-65 (R2)," Headquarters, 39th Transportation Battalion (Truck), APO San Francisco 96308, 4 May 1971.

[114] 1LT Daniel E. Ross, PL 512th TC, Letter of Commendation to the Commanding Officer, 359th Transportation Company, 19 March 1971.

585th Transportation Company

Wayne Chalker wrote an account of an armored unit escorting his convoy through an ambush. The important factor is that the tanks and APCs remained with the convoy and did not abandon it to chase after the enemy. The steep jungle terrain gave them no other choice. One might also notice that there was a tank or APC between each truck. That provided enough fire power to beat back most determined attacks. This type of escort was only practical because of the high probability of enemy ambush.

"THE FIRE BASE BASTOGNE CONVOY 4/68"[115]
Wayne Chalker
585th Transportation Company

During the week of April 12, 1968 eight members of the 585th Transportation Co. (Medium Truck Cargo) 39th Transportation Battalion, volunteered for a mission to bring much needed ammunition and gun barrels into FB Bastogne from their base camp at Phu Bai. This is the story from three of the eight who took part in this convoy.

On January 14, 1968, headquarters, maintenance, and 2nd platoon of the 585th were loaded onto LST 551 in Qui Nhon harbor and sailed for Da Nang for ultimate relocation to Camp Eagle, 101st AB base camp, Phu Bai. The remainder of the 585th would join the lead elements sometime in March 1968 following the same procedure.

Prior to the 585th's redeployment to Phu Bai in I Corps, the 585th was part of the 27th Trans Battalion running convoys to exotic places like An Khe, Pleiku, Dak To, Bong Son, Phu Cat, etc from their base camp at Phu Tai in II Corps.

The 585th was a 5ton tractor-trailer unit. Like most transportation companies in Vietnam, we were self sufficient and very mobile. We were a very close company and depended on each other very much.

In mid April 1968, Sgt. Edwards, our 1st Platoon Sgt., asked for volunteers for a convoy. Eight members volunteered to the best of our knowledge. Four of these volunteers were Wayne C Chalker, Marion Amos, Steve Plummer, and James McGrath.

Sgt. Edwards would not tell us where we were going, but told us to be ready the next morning. "Never before had we ever been asked to volunteer."[116] "We were loaded with artillery projectiles and black powder at the Phu Bai ammo dump."[117] At least two of us, Marion Amos and me, were loaded with 175mm howitzer barrels.

"The 101st guys seemed surprised that none of us had assistant drivers with us. I stated that our company was always under strength and that we always drove by ourselves. He told me that where you guys are going, you need to have someone riding shotgun with

---

[115] Army Transportation Association Vietnam, 134.198.33.115/atav/default.html.
[116] Steve Plummer, personal account.
[117] Steve Plummer, personal account.

you, especially with black powder because 'Charlie' gets nervous when he sees this ammo coming toward him. I really didn't know what he meant at the time."[118]

We were going to Fire Base Bastogne which was at the mouth of the A Shau Valley. FB Bastogne conducted fire support missions for units operating mostly in and around the A Shau Valley. FB Bastogne was located west of Phu Bai in Thua Thien Province. We were going to be the first convoy from our company to attempt a resupply of FB Bastogne.

"The eight tractor-trailers were lead from the ammo dump through Camp Eagle and into the countryside by a 101st AB jeep. The farther we drove, the heavier the jungle became. I thought it was unusual that there were no civilians in the area. We went around a bend in the road and met up with tanks and APC's that were interspersed with our trucks. I started to worry and put on my helmet and flak jacket."[119]

The OIC of the armor advised us that we would have escort for the last mile or so into FB Bastogne. He stated the left side of the road was under 101st control, while the right side was not. The OIC also told us NOT to stop under any circumstances or we would simply be pushed off the road by the armor in back of that truck.

"The road was turning into a steep narrow path with jungle growing up to the edge of this so called road. In II Corp convoys through 'Ambush Alley', we were told to keep lots of space between trucks so to lessen the effects of an ambush. With this in mind, I dropped back from the APC in front of me. A soldier from the armor behind me ran up and said I was going to get all of our asses shot off if I didn't stay close to the other APC. It then struck me that our survival depended on firepower from the armor."[120] This so-called road, which turned into a path through the jungle, had several steep hills before ending at Bastogne. "Because of the steepness on one hill and my overloaded trailer, I was pushed by an APC."[121]

"Suddenly, all hell broke loose."[122] The armor opened up with everything they had on the ride side of the road. "The noise was incredible. I started seeing red flashes flying over the hood of my truck and exploding on the other side of the road. I could also see small arms fire hitting hear me. I panicked and almost jumped from my truck into the jungle for cover. I'm sure this would have ended everything for those and me in the armor and trucks behind. The Army taught us that you always try and drive through an ambush. Somehow, I got down as low as I could behind the wheel and kept driving. Believing that I was about to die, I remember thinking about how bad my parents were going to feel, and I started to pray."[123]

In my truck, I remember the intense firing, but I also remember that I had to get my truck up and over each hill in front of me. Survival, in my mind, was to stay close to the tank in

---

[118] Steve Plummer, personal account.
[119] Steve Plummer, personal account.
[120] Steve Plummer, personal account.
[121] Steve Plummer, personal account.
[122] Steve Plummer, personal account.
[123] Steve Plummer, personal account.

front of me. As mentioned before, I was carrying 175mm howitzer barrels. The weight was far too heavy for my 5-ton tractor. While going up one steep hill, I reached '1st under' in a very short time. Even at 1st under, I felt my Rpm's drop.

As I neared the crest of this hill, even over the firing, I knew something happened to my engine. The thought of being pushed off the road by the APC behind me was frightening. I said a prayer and miraculously my engine held out to the top of the hill.

Not long after, all our trucks made it safety into FB Bastogne. "The guys who unloaded us at Bastogne seemed surprised we arrived intact. One asked me if I had any RPG's fired at me. I said I don't know, what are those? He said they would have been red flashes and explosions after they hit. I said yes, several and I wondered what those were. They also asked which side of the road the incoming fire came from. I said the left. They told me that the left side was supposed to be secure."[124]

Having never been to a firebase like Bastogne before, I got a bad feeling about this place and was very anxious to get unloaded and back on the road again. The jungle came right up to the perimeter of the base. Sort of like an island in the middle of the Pacific.

We were hurrying to get unloaded and regroup for our fun drive back, when the Major (OIC) informed us the road back has been closed. Just prior to this, Steve remembered a small convoy of duce and a half's leaving Bastogne just after we arrived and escorted by the same armor that brought us in. It was rumored that this convoy was hit hard going down the same road we just came up.

The OIC told us to spread out our trucks in the firebase so we would be a smaller target. The Major also advised us to be ready to move out on 15-minute notice. We were to remain at Bastogne for the next six days waiting for the road to be re secured by the 101st.

We were obviously unprepared for our unscheduled stopover at Bastogne. None of us had any change of clothes, food, personal hygiene items, or extra ammunition. During the week, we experienced what life was really like at a firebase. "Sitting and waiting all those days, I'd see jets dive and drop napalm near the perimeter or on the hillsides."9.

We caught up on much needed sleep during this week. I remember pulling guard duty with a 101st guy and trading hand grenades with him. I had the newer, baseball type and he had the older oval style. (In addition to our personal issued weapons, 585th members carried hand grenades in their trucks). During the week, the base ammo dump blew. "We jumped into bunkers with the 101st people. The ammo was still going off when I saw at least four medics with stretchers running towards it. I think that was the bravest thing I ever saw. No one must have been hurt because when it was all over, they walked back."[125]

---

[124] Steve Plummer, personal account.
[125] Steve Plummer, personal account.

On or about April 24th, the Major told us to pack up and get ready to move out in 15minutes. Our stay at Bastogne was ending. We were happy to be leaving and getting back to base camp, but were fearful of what lie ahead. "Many of us were worried about the road back, and I remember some of us were saying good bye to our friends just in case."[126]

The return convoy was set up similar to the one we came in with a week earlier, tank, truck, APC, truck, etc. I remember the Major asking us if we could assist his armor with suppression fire on the left side of the road. I thought this odd, as all of us know it is hard to shoot and drive at the same time.

Soon after leaving Bastogne, the firing commenced again. The intensity was the same as coming in the week before. I remember several explosions on the edge of the road to our left. I was doing my best to fire out the window and steer at the same time. I remember shell casings from my M-14 burning my left arm.

"We left the fire base and started driving down the mountain when all hell broke loose. The tanks and APC's opened fire and we started shooting to the left of the road. I had my rifle cradled in my left arm and I was shooting out the driver's side window. It was a real challenge shifting gears and shooting out the window and not running into the back of the APC in front of me. When one magazine emptied, I would put in another and keep firing."[127]

"After checking my forward movement, I looked to the left, and continued to fire my weapon. This is when I thought the devil himself had just hit me between the eyes with his fist. My head jolted and snapped back. My black plastic rim glasses were shoved back and down into my nose. The pain of being hit between the eyes was excruciating. I thought my nose was broke. I wasn't sure what happened. So many things run through your mind. First, I thought I must have hit a pothole and bumped my head on the steering wheel. When I looked up, everything was black. I looked around and saw nothing but darkness. A few seconds passed and my vision returned. Everything happened so fast that I was in a state of confusion for a moment. After realizing I didn't hit a pothole, I gathered my thoughts, pushed my glasses back up on my nose and kept shooting and driving. The only thing on my mind again was to get out of that area as quick as we could."[128]

Marion's truck was ahead of mine in the convoy back. As I previously mentioned, I remember several explosions just in front of my truck on the left edge of the road. One of these explosions would have been in line with the driver's side of Marion's truck. When we cleared the fire zone area, the armor pulled out and we pulled off and stopped to regroup. Marion came walking back to me and had blood streaming down his face from a hole in his forehead just above the rim of his glasses.

[126] Steve Plummer, personal account.
[127] Marion Amos, personal account.
[128] Marion Amos, personal account.

He had obviously been hit with shrapnel and it had been deflected off the center portion of his glasses. This may have saved his live or at least prevented a more serious wound. I knew we had to get out of this area as quickly as possible. We were still in hostile territory without any armor or convoy protection.

I sat Marion down and bandaged him as best I could and asked him if he could drive. He said he could. I told him to stay in front of me so I could watch him until be arrived back at Phu Bai which was 10-15 miles away. In addition to no convoy protection, we had no radio and no OIC.

The convoy into Bastogne the week before began to take its toll on our trucks. "We all knew that this area was unsafe and everyone wanted out of there as fast as possible, but more trucks started breaking down. I think we may have had up to four trucks no longer running by the time we got back to Phu Bai. We came in pushing and pulling each other at about 5miles per hour. No one was left behind. We all came back together."'"[129]

When we arrived back at Phu Bai, I escorted Marion to an aid station. The medic examined him, re bandaged him and told him to go back to work. Several days later, Marion experienced severe headaches and returned to a Maine aid station. There he was re examined and some shrapnel was removed from his forehead.

Marion, to this day, carries a small piece of shrapnel in his head from that day.

Nothing more was ever said to the eight from that convoy. We all went back to work the next day hauling to Camp Evans, Quang Tri, Dong Ha etc. No one, to our knowledge, ever received any award or commendation for our volunteer mission into Bastogne.

Marion never received a Purple Heart. It may be that we were not deserving of any recognition, but Marion should have his Purple Heart.

After 34years, the three of us have found each other thanks to the Internet and ATAV! We are still searching for the other members of the 'Bastogne Convoy'. God willing, someday we will find them and learn even more about that week in April 1968.

Marion is making attempts to get his military medical records for his Purple Heart and health care, which he never received, from the VA. All of us have submitted applications for corrections of military records for consideration for any awards we may have been denied.

Marion lives in Colorado and works for Coors, Steve lives in Minnesota and works for the Postal Service, and I live in Maine and work for the Bureau of Customs and Border Protection.

The above story is as accurate as our collective memories will allow. All three of us recognize the heroic acts of many, many others truckers in Vietnam and the supreme

[129] Marion Amos, personal account.

sacrifice many combat truckers made during the course of that war. Our story pales in comparison to the hundreds more trucker stories during that conflict.

Lam Son 719

By 1970, the gun truck design and doctrine had reached fruition. Experimentation had ended. The 523rd Transportation Company (Medium Truck) had six gun trucks; Satan's Lil' Angel, Ace of Spades, Black Widow, Uncle Meat, King Kong and Eve of Destruction. Each of the three platoons had two gun trucks. By then, new crew members were volunteers selected by consensus of the other crew members. The gun truck crews felt elite but the 523rd believed that by assigning two gun trucks to each platoon, rather than to their own platoon, they felt more like members of the company. They lived with the drivers who they had to protect. Since they were the best, much was expected of them and if they failed to defend the trucks then they would have to face their brothers when they returned to the barracks at night.

This late in the war, there was a shortage of Transportation Corps officers. Second lieutenants made first lieutenant in one year then captain in the next. The rapid promotion and other duties caused a shortage of lieutenants in the truck companies. The burden of leading convoys fell heavily on the NCOs. However, during 1970, the Army assigned three infantry officers to the 523rd. 1LT Ralph Fuller had recently served in the 25th Infantry Division but when it was inactivated, he still had part of his one-year tour to complete, so he was assigned to the 523rd. 2LTs Jim Baird and Tom Callahan had both graduated from OCS 2-70 and were assigned directly to the 523rd. The only logical reason they could conclude why the Army assigned infantry officers to truck companies were the gun trucks. This hinted that the Army felt that gun trucks were a combat arms mission. For whatever reason they were assigned there, the officers identified with the gun trucks and loved the men who crewed them. As combat arms officers they felt their place was on the road. Many preferred to ride in the gun trucks, endearing them with the crews.[130]

CPT Donald Voightritter commanded the company. He was a fair and respected officer. His brother Ronald, another TC officer, had already earned the Silver Star Medal for valor. The personality of commanders defines the character of their commands. Voightritter created an atmosphere of mutual respect and camaraderie. This was the strongest asset of the company. The officers would discuss informally with the gun truck crews what they had done during ambushes. No two ambushes were the same and the gun truck crews reacted differently to each one. These discussions inspired confidence with the lieutenants in their crews.

In January 1970, the 523rd was sent north from its home in Cha Rang Valley to Phu Bai along the coastal Highway 1 in the I Corps Tactical Zone in preparation for Operation Lam Son 719. Gathered intelligence indicated that the North Vietnamese Army was building up their logistic bases across the Laotian border in preparation for an offensive. MACV felt that by attacking the logistic base closest to the North Vietnamese would

---

[130] Jeffrey Fuller interview by Richard Killblane, June 2004, Jim Baird interview by Richard Killblane, 20 June 2005.

disrupt the preparations and delay or discourage the attack. Congress had passed a law after the US Cambodian incursion that prevented US ground troops from crossing the border again. The Army of the Republic of Vietnamese (ARVN) would cross the border with the support of US helicopters and artillery. The artillery set up their fire base at the abandoned Marine camp, Khe Sanh. The 39th Transportation Battalion had the responsibility to supply the forward deployed troops. The east-west, Route 9 was the supply route and the battalion posted two 5-ton cargo truck companies at Camp Vandergrift.[131]

To weaken American support to the ARVN drive into Laos, the NVA likewise struck at American supply line with the intent to completely shut it down. Two areas lent themselves to ideal ambush areas, Route 9 and Hi Van Pass along Highway 1. During the two and a half month operation, the NVA conducted 23 convoy ambushes along Route 9.

The road to Vandergrift was a two-lane paved road through a valley of tall elephant grass. From there, a narrow, single lane, unimproved dirt road snaked along the ridge with a river 50 to 100 feet below. The demand for supplies required the two truck companies to deliver cargo around the clock, day and night. To prevent driving off the road at night, the trucks rolled with their lights on giving the enemy ample warning of their arrival. The steep slopes with thick jungle vegetation growing right up to the road made this ideal ambush terrain. During Lam Son, the guerrillas stepped up the frequency and ferocity of their attacks ambushes hoping to starve off the American support.

20 February 1971

523rd Transportation Company, 39th Transportation Battalion

2LT Baird had been sent back to Phu Bai to pick up 17 brand new 5-ton trucks. They returned after dark. The convoy doctrine at the time was to limit convoys to no more than 30 trucks with a gun truck ratio of 1:10. Uncle Meat led the convoy with King Kong in the middle and Satan's Lil' Angel in the rear. All gun trucks had three M2 .50 caliber machineguns. The M2 .50 was the most successful design in American weapons and had seen very little change in its design since its original issue in 1919. This time Baird rode close to the rear in a ¾-ton gun beep with twin M60 machineguns. He noticed that some Transportation Corps officers preferred to ride up front. He knew that if there was trouble it would invariably occur in the rear and that is where the key decisions would have to be made. If an ambush split the convoy, by doctrine the trucks out of the kill zone would continue to role of to the next security check point or camp. If the convoy commander was in the lead then the commander in would be unable to make the key decisions for the rest of the convoy either trapped in the kill zone or behind. 1LT David R. Wilson was killed trying to reenter the kill zone in an unprotected jeep.[132]

---

[131] LTC Alvin C. Ellis, "Operational Report – Lessons Learned, 39th Transportation Battalion (Truck), Period Ending 30 April 1971, RCS CSFOR-65 (R2)," Headquarters, 39th Transportation Battalion (Truck), APO San Francisco 96308, 4 May 1971.

[132] Baird interview and Danny Cochran interview by Richard Killblane, 18 June 2005.

It was dark as the convoy neared Camp Vandergrift. The mountain ridge to the south came within yards of Highway 9 and a valley of tall elephant grass covered the valley to the ridge line to the north. Within a mile and a half of their destination, Baird heard an explosion followed by an intense volume of small arms fire from the jungle on the ridge to his left. Two RPG had struck Satan's Lil' Angel's gun box and the right front tire. An RPG had struck Satan's Lil' Angel's gun box from the north side of the road, killing right rear gunner, SP4 Richard B. Frazier, and wounded left rear gunner and NCOIC, SGT Chester Israel. Small arms fire shot out the tires of the gun truck. The NVA had learned to take out the gun trucks first before they went after the rest of the trucks. Without a crew to fire back, the driver of Satan's Lil' Angel drove his truck on rims out of the kill zone.[133]

Baird raced ahead and passed a disabled 5-ton cargo truck in the ditch. He ordered his driver to stop so they could check on the driver. They came to a halt a hundred feet ahead of the truck. He did not want to leave the disabled truck until he was sure that its driver was safe. To do so required him to wait in the middle of the kill zone. As soon as his gunner tried to return fie, both M60s failed to fire. Cochran heard someone say that the gas plugs had been put in backwards. Evidently, someone had put the gas plugs in backwards when it was reassembled them. Evidently, he had put the gas plugs in backwards when he reassembled them. The three men only had one M79 grenade launcher and their M16s to defend against an NVA company. Baird immediately radioed the two lead gun trucks and told them to come back. The one thing that Baird could depend on was the loyalty of his gun truck to rescue him or any other truck in trouble.

Neither the crew of Uncle Meat nor King Kong had heard the gun fire behind them. The majority of the convoy had continued to Vandergrift as nothing had happened. Uncle Meat had already entered the compound and King Kong had just made the right hand turn into Vandergrift when they heard Baird's call for help. Immediately backed up, turned around and raced as fast as their trucks would let them back to the kill zone.[134]

Baird knew his gun truck crews and had confidence in their judgment. He also knew that too much jabber on the radio would cause confusion and tie up the radio net. He quickly and precisely informed the gun trucks of the situation. Satan's Lil' Angel had been hit, his gun beep and one 5-ton were still in the kill zone. The crews asked which side of the road the enemy was on and Baird informed them that he was taking small arms fire from the ridge to his south and the field of elephant grass to his north. The enemy was close enough to throw hand grenades at his vehicle. He then quit talking. He would count on their judgment as what to do.[135]

Ten minutes of steady small arms fire had elapsed since the beginning of the ambush. By then Baird was taking fire from both sides of the road. Enemy was closing in from the elephant grass while others fired down on them from the ridge to the south. His gunner, Downer, tapped him on the shoulder and said, "I see one. What do I do?" Baird turned,

[133] Baird interview.
[134] Baird and Cochran interview.
[135] Baird and Cochran interview.

looked back down the road and saw an enemy soldier about ten yards away on a berm alongside the road loading an RPG. He told his gunner to shoot him. The gunner fired his M79 grenade launcher at him. The enemy soldier was close for the 40mm grenade to arm in flight. It struck him with enough velocity to either kill or incapacitate him, because he did not fire his rocket.[136]

Around ten minutes after the initiation of the ambush, King Kong raced up to their convoy commander's ¾-ton, parking right in front of it at a 45 degree angle facing to the north. Uncle Meat similarly parked near Satan's Lil' Angel. Baird was never as glad as when he saw the tracers of those .50s. There was a reassurance that everything would turn out alright. He knew his gun truck crews knew what to do. Baird called on the radio, "They're in the ditches. They're in the ditches." The gunners on the Kong swung their .50s around and sprayed the ditches.[137]

The success of an ambush depended upon surprise and extreme violence. The gun truck crews had learned to turn the fight back on the enemy as fast as they could with even more violence. This would take the psychological advantage away from the enemy forcing them to break contact. The .50s blazed away in four to six round bursts at the muzzle flashes to their left and right. The gunners poured 30-weight oil from plastic canteens to help cool the barrels and ensure the smooth function of their breaches after firing off about three to four boxes of ammunition.[138]

An RPG hit the rear duals right and exploded in all the colors of the rainbow under left rear gunner, Danny Cochran, knocking him backwards on Larson manning the right .50. Cochran then jumped back up, grabbed his .50 and went back to work. King Kong was an APC gun truck. Large chunks of hot shrapnel had come up through the aluminum floor of the hull and lodged in the top of the box right under his machinegun. One piece of shrapnel had burnt a hole in the charging handle and others had left five or six holes in the barrel, but it still fired.[139]

The barrels turned red and as soon as the gunners saw the rounds curve after they left the barrel they knew it was time to change them. Each time Emery, manning the turret gun, swung his barrel toward Cochran, Cochran grabbed the asbestos glove, spun the barrel off then picked up a new barrel and spun it on tight, by feel counted three clicks back and let go. Gunners had different methods of setting the headspace and timing and none used the timing gage during an ambush. They knew their guns. Some memorized the number of clicks for each breach. Others wrote the number of clicks needed on each barrel. Cochran did it by feel. He backed off the three clicks and depending upon the rate of fire of his .50 he added more clicks. He knew his .50. He changed two barrels for the TC and one for himself that night.[140]

---

[136] Baird and Cochran interview.
[137] Baird and Cochran interview.
[138] Cochran interview.
[139] Cochran interview.
[140] Cochran interview.

The one advantage to fighting at night, the gunners fired in the direction of the enemy muzzle flashes, which betrayed their positions. There was no concealment in the dark once one fired his weapon.

The tactic worked. After about ten minutes of firing, Uncle Meat and King Kong had turned the fight back on the enemy and they broke contact. During the fight, the driver of the disabled 5-ton had run to his convoy commander's vehicle. That close to Vandergrift, Uncle Meat loaded the wounded from Satan's Lil' Angel into their gun truck then drove off the road and backed up to Baird's vehicle. The drive shaft had broken and the vehicle could not drive. The crew of Uncle Meat hooked up the ¾-ton to Uncle Meat, which towed it into Vandergrift. After the initial volley of fire, no other casualties were taken. King Kong limped back to Vandergrift on its rims.[141]

Lesson

The success of the ambush depended upon a number of factors. First and foremost, the dedication and determination of the gun truck crews. Without hesitation the two lead gun trucks raced back into the kill zone. The convoy commanders knew their men and trusted in their judgment to do the right thing in an ambush. This allowed Baird to keep his radio transmission short and to the point, keeping the net free for important traffic. Too much chatter would prevent someone from interjecting important information at the critical time. Each of the gun trucks instinctively raced to a disabled vehicle to provide covering fire. Failure to test fire the M60s, however, failed to warn the gunner of the ¾-ton that he had reassembled them wrong. On the other hand, the intimate knowledge of the gunners with their .50s caused them to fire none stop for ten minutes. The .50 caliber round could penetrate through most trees and bunkers and cut a man in half if it struck him. The hail of six .50s inspired fear in the NVA and caused the enemy to break contact.

12 March 1971

39th Transportation Battalion

A narrow, single lane, unimproved dirt road snaked its way along a ridge from Forward Support Base Vandergrift to Khe Sanh with a river 50 to 100 feet below. Because the road past Vandergrift could only support 2 ½ and 5-ton cargo trucks, the 39th Battalion would need another light truck company to push from Vandergrift to Khe Sanh. The thick jungle that grew right up to the road made it ideal for ambushes and the fact that convoys had to run both day and night made ambushes easier. The 1st Brigade, 5th Mechanized Infantry Division had responsibility for the security of that section of the road.

On 12 March, 2LT Jim Baird, Platoon Leader of 523rd Transportation Company, led a convoy from Vandergrift to Khe Sanh. Just in case the enemy tried to ambush a convoy, the detail left behind kept a reaction force. 1LT Ralph Fuller, another platoon leader, had all the gun trucks lined up ready to go.[142]

---

[141] Cochran interview.
[142] Fuller interview.

A B-40 rocket hit the gun truck, Proud America, between the cab and the gun box on the driver's side mortally wounding the driver, SP4 Robert W. Thorne. Thorne steered the truck into the hillside instead of down the steep cliff into the creek. This saved the rest of the crew. Unfortunately, Baird had been kneeling by the radio mounted in the left front corner of the box when the rocket hit. He received multiple fragmentary wounds and lost his left arm.[143]

Fuller heard the call, "contact, contact, contact," on the radio and led his convoy of gun trucks. He rode in the Daughter of Darkness. An engineer stopped him saying that there was an ambush up the road. They drove past. 2LT Tom Callahan, another platoon leader, laid Baird on a stretcher and drove him to a better location near the bridge for the medevac helicopter to land. The helicopter arrived but was afraid to land, instead, the men lifted the stretcher up to the bird. Fuller told the medevac crew, "Take care of him. He was a good one." They placed Thorne's body in the Black Widow and took it back to Vandergrift.[144]

3. Southern II Corps Tactical Zone

500th Transportation Group, Cam Ranh Bay

In spite of the losses incurred in the Central Highlands by 8th Group convoys, the 500th Group had not lost anyone to an ambush until late 1969, almost two years after the ambushes began along Route 19. The threat level was not nearly as dangerous as it was on Route 19 though enemy attacks on convoys in the southern II Corps Zone began to increase in the summer and fall of 1969. In response, the 36th Battalion began constructing gun trucks. At first they built double wall gun boxes out of lumber with the air gap filled with sandbags. These turned out to be too heavy resulting in poor handling, excessive wear on the tires and continuous brake failures and resulted in the death of one driver. These were replaced with 5/8-inch steel walls.[145]

The 36th Transportation Battalion had three truck companies: the 442nd Medium Truck, 566th Medium Truck and the 670th Medium Truck. The 670th had the 32nd Transportation Platoon which hauled refrigeration or "reefer" vans. The 360th Transportation Company (POL), although belonging to the Quartermaster battalion, rode in the 36th Battalion convoys. The 360th Medium Truck Company had built three gun trucks: USA in the 1st Platoon, Roach Coach in the 2nd Platoon and Scrogin's Heroes in the 3rd Platoon. The 442nd Medium Truck built the Flying Dutchman, Widow Maker (?) and Ejaculator.[146]

April 1969

36th Transportation Battalion

In late April 1969, a convoy from the 36th Battalion was bound for the 2/1 Cavalry base camp at Phan Rang south along the coastal highway (QL1). This was a short run that

143 Fuller interview.

144 Fuller interview.

145 MAJ Thomas P. Storey, "Operational Report – Lessons Learned, Headquarters, 36th Transportation Battalion, Period Ending 17 January 1970." Headquarters, 36th Transportation Battalion (Truck) APO 96312, 17 January 1970.

146 Ronald Smith interview by Richard Killblane, 17 June 2005 and Wayne Patrick interview by Richard Killblane, 12 July 2002.

only took half a day to reach the destination and then return by the end of the day. The convoys ran with 70 to 80 trucks with three to five gun trucks. They usually had an MP gun jeep or V-100 armored car in the lead and gun trucks spaced evenly throughout the convoy with one in the trail party. The line up consisted of the MP gun jeep, the convoy commander's gun jeep, Rick "Snuffy" Smith's gun jeep, then the cargo trucks.[147]

Route 1 or QL 1 ran north and south along the flat coastal plane. The "Coconut Grove," was about halfway between Cam Ranh Bay and Phan Rang to the south. The "Coconut Grove" was a rubber plantation on the west side of the road and open field on the east with elephant grass. Smith claimed that a million monkeys must have lived in the grove and swarmed the trucks whenever they passed. That is why they called it the "Coconut Grove." The coastal highway was a heavily trafficked highway by both military and civilian traffic. For this reason, no one ever expected to get hit along this route. The drivers did not even wear their flak vests.[148]

When the convoy reached the "Coconut Grove," the enemy initiated the ambush with small arms fire on the lead and middle vehicles creating two kill zones. The APC gun truck, "USA," and one gun jeep were caught off guard. There was one gun truck and one gun jeep for every 30 vehicles. The vehicles were typically bunched up with no more than 20 feet between vehicles. The lead kill zone caught 16-20 vehicles. Gun trucks did their normal routine. Rick Smith fired his M79 grenade launcher from the hip as fast as could. The enemy fired a few mortars but missed. They overshot. The fire fight lasted about 15 minutes.[149]

No one in the convoy was killed or wounded but a number of vehicles were shot up. Most of them had flat tires. All were able to drive to their destination. The thing that Rick Smith learned was to never take his eyes off Coconut Grove again.[150]

Lesson
Expect an ambush where you would normally least expect it. The enemy watches the convoy behavior and looks for signs of weakness.

October/November 1969
36th Transportation Battalion
Ban Me Thout was a routine destination for the 36th Battalion. The terrain between Nha Trang and Ban Me Thout was mountainous jungle with some open areas where the jungle had been cleared or defoliated. The road was so narrow that trucks could not pass. The run to Ban Me Thout took most of the day so the convoys had to RON at the camp and return the next day. The convoys ran with anywhere from 80 to 150 vehicles divided into serials of 20 30 vehicles with a 5 to 10 minute gap between them. An MP with a V-100 armored car usually led each serial followed by a lieutenant or NCO in a gun jeep with radio communications and an M-60 mounted on a pedestal. Each serial had a Gun Truck

[147] Rick Smith telephone interview by Richard Killblane, 22 August 2005.
[148] Ronald Smith and Rick Smith interviews.
[149] Ronald Smith and Ronald Smith interviews.
[150] Rick Smith Interview.

with an NCO, radio and one 50 Caliber machine gun and two M-60. The Trail Party made up the last serial and included a gun jeep, wrecker, Medic Ambulance, tire truck, 10 to 20 bob tails and gun truck. The number of extra bob tails depended on the size of the convoy. Because of the rapid promotion from second lieutenant to captain in two years, LTC Edward Honor, the 36th Battalion Commander, had a policy that captains had to be the convoy commanders.[151]

Around October or November 1969, CPT Wayne Patrick, Commander of the 442nd Medium Truck Company, was the convoy commander. On a return trip from Ban Me Thout, the convoy was delayed on account of the poor weather conditions and low clouds prevented helicopters from flying. Normally the convoys departed between 0700 to 0800 hours depending on mechanical problems. After line-up for the return trip they waited around an hour or more for the weather to improve. LTC Honor also had a policy that no convoy would run without air cover. It would have been normal procedure to radio Battalion headquarters and inform them of the situation and get approval. Air cover would normally have joined them before they had gone far outside Ban Me Thout. CPT Patrick made the decision to depart without air cover since road security in the mountain pass was considered adequate.[152]

The 101st Airborne Division and ROK Army provided security in the area. The Koreans had a base at the top of the Pass and the ARVN had a training base at the bottom. CPT Patrick had radio contact with security operations when entering there area of operation and there had been no reports of any significant enemy activity. It was not unusual to receive sporadic small arms fire from time to time but no convoy had been ambushed on this route before. Another factor in making the decision to depart was to return to Cam Ranh Bay before dark. It was not unusual to delay departure for various reasons but it was unusual to cancel a return trip.[153]

An MP V-100 armored car and a gun jeep lead the convoy. The convoy had between 80 and 100 vehicles divided into serials. CPT Patrick kept a gun truck at the rear of the first serial another in the trail party and the others space evenly though the middle of the convoy. He often rode either in the rear of the first serial or the middle of the convoy. This day he rode in the middle. This allowed him to drive up and down the convoy to respond better to problems. It also kept him in radio range with the lead and rear of his convoy. As the convoy commander, CPT Patrick's jeep had three radios to coordinate with air, ground and artillery support.[154]

About two hours after departure, the convoy was halfway down the mountain pass in the area secured by the 101st Airborne Division The mountain rose above them on the north side of the road, to their left, and leveled out into a flat cleared zone to the south (their

[151] Wayne Patrick email to Richard Killblane, August 29, 2005. LTG Edward Honor remembered that the gap between serials was 10-15 minutes. Edward Honor email to Richard Killblane, August 31, 2005. Wayne Patrick remembered that the gap was 4-6 minutes, Wayne Patrick Email to Richard Killblane, September 1, 2005.
[152] Patrick email.
[153] Patrick interview, 12 July 2002 and 17 June 2005 and email August 29, 2005.
[154] Patrick interview, 12 July 2002 and 17 June 2005.

right) with a tree line around 100 yards away. That section of paved road had multiple curves that caused the trucks to slow down. CPT Patrick heard a boom up ahead followed by the report of contact on the radio.[155]

The enemy in the wood line fired three to five B40 rockets (RPGs) at one of the gun trucks in the middle of the convoy and hit the top corner of the passenger side of gun box. The blast wounded three crew members and cut Don Matthews in half. The lead part of the convoy continued on while the trucks behind stopped. Another gun truck pulled security on the disabled gun truck. The fight lasted five minutes.[156]

CPT Patrick was a quarter to a half a mile behind it and raced up to the rear of the disabled gun truck. He reached the scene a few minutes later. He was on the radio with the 101st. A couple of 101st troops were nearby and were firing on the tree line for another 15 to 20 minutes. In just a few minutes there was a call on his radio from a Cobra Gun Ship, with the call sign "Undertaker." He reported his position and three Cobras came in and worked the area over for about ten minutes. During that time, a Huey from the101st Airborne Division came in and extracted the wounded. The rest of the convoy continued on. The trail party recovered the disabled gun truck.[157]

The rest of the convoy moved up while the area was secure and the trail party secured the disabled gun truck. The rear half of the convoy regrouped with the lead half at the normal rest stop in a safe area. The convoy returned to Cam Ranh Bay without further incident.[158]

Lessons learned

"It was standard operating procedure to have air cover. Although we had sporadic enemy contact when air cover was in the area it was a deterrent to enemy activity. Radio communications within the convoy and with area security forces were extremely important. Quick response from area security forces limited the enemy's ability to continue with the attack. The Convoy Commander needs to be in the middle of the convoy to be able to respond quickly. The convoy maintained security and cleared the kill zone as per normal instructions. Clearing the contact/kill zone was always covered in briefings with convoy officers and NCO's. Drivers and others on the convoy knew to clear contact/kill zone.[159]

"Lessons you could learn from this ambush. (1) Have air cover up or very close by (2) Have security forces on notice for quick response, make radio contact (3) The Convoy Commander should have more than one radio, one to run the convoy and one for air support or security forces. (4) You should have multiple Gun Trucks or armored vehicles per convoy in order to protect and secure the convoy in the event of attack or multiple attacks. (5) Briefings should be held prior to departing to ensure that all personnel are aware of critical instructions to follow in the event of an attack. (6) Make sure your

---

[155] Patrick email, August 29, 2005.
[156] Patrick interview, 12 July 2002 and 17 June 2005.
[157] Patrick interview, 12 July 2002 and 17 June 2005 and email, August 29, 2005.
[158] Patrick email, August 29, 2005.
[159] Patrick email, August 29, 2005.

weapons work prior to departure, test fire your weapons. This wasn't a problem for the 442 but based on my discussion with you in Branson I thought I would add this one."[160]

26 June 1970

360th Transportation Company (POL), 262nd Quartermaster Battalion

A normal line haul mission to Ban Me Thout had 80 to 120 vehicles. Ronald Smith remembered the convoy on 26 June 1970 had 12 gun trucks; four from the 360th POL Company, four from the 670th Medium Truck Company and four from the 442nd Medium Truck. The Reefers were in front, followed by the flat beds with projectiles (projos) and food, then POL tankers and the trail party. Convoys were organized by type of truck then by company. This would have placed the 360th POL tankers in the last march unit of the convoy.[161]

SSG Jack Buckwalter was the NCOIC of the 360th march unit. It started out with 21 vehicles. The platoon leader was the convoy serial commander and rode in a gun jeep at the head of the serial with a MP V-100 and a gun truck. Another gun truck rode closer to the rear. A gun truck and three more gun jeeps were even distributed through the serial. SSG Buckwalter rode in the trail gun jeep at the end of the convoy. This was the policy of 500th Group convoys at the time. Ten 10-ton tractor and trailers loaded with petaprime were waiting for them at the bottom of the Ban Me Thout Pass so they could have air cover going up the Pass. The convoy had an L-19 Birddog for air cover. The ten tractors and trailers fell in the last serial.[162]

On its way up the Ban Me Thout Pass, an enemy soldier fired an RPG at one of the lead POL tankers driven by SP4 Charles Pedigo. The rocket flew at an angle through the cab and hit the fuel tank. Smith remembered that Pedigo safely jumped out of the cab but the truck started to roll forward. He jumped back in the cab to set the hand brake then the fuel tanker blew up killing the driver. That act prevented the truck from rolling back down the steep grade into the other trucks and blocking the pass. The burning truck melted to the asphalt. The burning tanker blocked the narrow mountain road stopping the convoy.[163]

The convoy commander and the vehicles ahead of the burning fuel tanker continued to Engineer Hill at the top of the Pass. He radioed back to his NCOIC that they were receiving small arms fire. They received small arms fire from the ridge across the valley to the north and down from the ridge above to the south. The enemy on the ridge across the valley had mortars and .51 caliber machineguns firing gray tracers. All the gun trucks entered the kill zone, pulled off to the side of the road and fired at the enemy on the opposite ridge. The air cover left because there was too much ground fire. One gun truck pulled up to right next to the burning tanker, the USA pulled over to the right side of the road about 300 meters below the burning tanker and returned fire [164]

---

[160] Patrick email, August 29, 2005.

[161] Ronald Smith interview by Richard Killblane, 17 June 2005 and Robert Dalton email to Richard Killblane, September 6, 2005.

[162] Jack Buckwalter telephone interview by Richard Killblane, 7 September 2005.

[163] Ronald Smith and Buckwalter interviews.

[164] Ronald Smith interview.

SSG Buckwalter only heard the muffled explosion of the rocket. He did not hear the small arms fires that far back in the convoy. He immediately raced his gun jeep to the front of the convoy. As he rounded the jungle road, he saw two MP gun jeeps halted on the left side of the road. He ordered them to drive up to the fight but they refused. Buckwater told his gunner to shoot them if they did not move. The MPs did as instructed. When the SSG reached the scene, there was no longer any enemy fire. He told the crews in the gun trucks to open fire anyway on the ridge across the valley. During the process, a major kept calling on the radio wanting to know about his petaprime.[165]

The gun trucks returned fire for 35 minutes until the firing quieted down. SSG Buckwalter then made the decision for the trucks behind it had to turn around and return down the mountain. The mountain road was narrow so "USA" had to back up to a place where the tractors could turn around. Smith could see the smoke for 35 miles. They found a MACV unit at the base of the hill and waited for two and a half hours until the lieutenant called that they had air cover again. The drivers did not like the idea of driving back up the hill but Buckwalter made them. On the trip up, he stopped to recover Pedigo's body from the burning truck. The body had been burnt into a small ball and a few bones. He did not see the skull, so he left it. The next day he stopped again but none of the body remained. Around 200 yards past the burned out tanker, the convoy was hit again by small arms fire but the gun trucks returned fire and the convoy kept going. The last gun truck dropped back to make sure that SSG Buckwalter was safe. It drove just ahead of the trial gun jeep the rest of the trip down the mountain.[166]

Lesson

This is one time that air cover did not discourage the enemy from attacking. The enemy attacked from the ridge across the valley. SSG Buckwalter thought the initial RPG round was first from the gully below the road. That is why it hit its target. The small arms fire may have been ineffective because of the range. Convoys had been hit several times in this location and the enemy seems to have tried attacking from different locations.

Since the enemy destroyed a fuel truck in the front part of the convoy, only the convoy commander and few vehicles were able to continue to safety. Fortunately, the most experienced leader was in the rear. SSG Buckwalter had already completed a couple tours in Vietnam. He was probably the most experienced soldier in the convoy serial. In this case placing the NCOIC in the rear of the convoy and the lieutenant at the head was a good idea. From atop the Pass, the lieutenant was able to get the air cover for the convoy to return.

36th Transportation Battalion, 500th Transportation Group

During another ambush at Ban Me Thout Pass, the enemy buried a satchel charge in the road which blew up the lead V-100. The gun trucks stayed and fought for 15 to 20 minutes then turned around.

---

165 Smith interview and Dalton email.

166 Buckwalter interview.

Lessons

Ban Me Thout Pass, like the two mountain passes along Route 19, provided ideal cover and concealment for the enemy to ambush convoys. While the gun trucks could anticipate an ambush in the Pass, they did not know exactly where or how. The enemy varied his tactics and the method of initiation. The rapid response by the gun trucks and security force usually limited the damage to just one vehicle.

36th Transportation Battalion, 500th Transportation Group

Rick Smith remembered that the worst attack happened between December 1969 and February 1970. Rick Smith was then the NCOIC of "Peace Maker" in the rear of the convoy. It did not have any radios. The trail party had only one gun truck. A wrecker rode two thirds of the way back in convoy.[167]

During an ambush the gun trucks in the kill zone would pull over and return fire. The next gun truck would pull up and relieve it, so it could return to its original place in the convoy. The last gun truck would fire until convoy was out of sight for 5-10 minutes. Rick's crew volunteered to be the last gun truck because they thought they were tough.[168]

Their destination was Ban Me Thuot, where the 101st Airborne Division had a base camp on top of mountain. They halted at bottom of mountain, then sent a spotter plane to check for enemy. It could not see anything since the enemy was hidden in the jungle. The convoy then received the word to proceed. An ARVN 2 ½-ton truck loaded with Vietnamese was hit coming down hill. The enemy had just shot the truck up with the passengers in the back. Blood was pouring out of it. Rick estimated that it had15 killed in the back. 75-100 yards further up ROK infantry and armor stopped their convoy. Then convoy commander sent a gun jeep back with instructions. The last four to five gun trucks were told to hang tight. They stayed back at 100-foot intervals while the convoy continued. They felt that the ROK could handle the enemy. Rick saw the ROKs running up the steep mountain. This impressed him. He heard lots of small arms fire and mortars. The convoy did not receive any hits. The mountain was too steep and the enemy was firing down over their heads. The gun trucks waited 15 minutes, then a ROK colonel came back and said he did not need them, so the gun trucks rejoined the convoy.[169]

When they arrived at the base camp, Rick saw American wounded stacked four deep in several ¾-ton trucks. They had been through a big fight. He did not think that that was a good way to treat wounded. He could not eat dinner that evening. The gun trucks when they RONed at a camp always pulled perimeter security. Gun trucks covered all the corners, ten feet from wire. At 0200, the "gooks" attacked the compound. The enemy reached the wire. Rick fired so many rounds that he had to change barrels twice. He did not use the timing gage. He just screwed the barrels in and back off three clicks. The

---

[167] Rick Smith interview.

[168] Rick Smith interview.

[169] Rick Smith interview.

infantry were so grateful they bought the gun truck crews breakfast the next day. He thinks the company received a citation for the action.[170]

4. III Corps Tactical Zone
48th Transportation Group

25 August 1968
7th Transportation Battalion
The 48th Transportation Group consisted of two battalions stationed at Long Binh in III Corps Tactical Zone. The 6th Battalion had all light truck companies and the 7th Battalion had all the medium truck companies. Long Binh cleared cargo from Saigon and the military terminal at Newport and delivered to base camps throughout the region. This southern part of the country gently sloped toward the Saigon and Mekong Rivers. Consequently, the unimproved roads that spread out from Long Binh and Saigon like the spokes of a wheel were flat and filled with pot holes.

25 August 1968 was a typical monsoon season day. The clouds hung low, making flying for helicopters dangerous, while intermittent hard rain drenched the area. A large resupply convoy of 81 trucks from the 48th Transportation Group departed Long Binh in three serials with six refrigeration trucks in the front, followed by cargo trucks, then fuel and ammunition trucks in the rear. If the enemy disabled a fuel or ammunition truck, the first half of the convoy would escape.[171]

The convoy proceeded west along Route 1 from Saigon past the 25th Infantry Division base camp at Cu Chi. There, the convoy divided into two serials and proceeded on to Go Dau Ha at the intersection of Route 1 and Route 22. The convoy then turned northwest onto Route 22 then through the village of Ap Nhi just 20 miles short of its destination at Tay Ninh. This convoy resupplied the 1st Brigade, 25th Infantry Division located just seven miles from the Cambodian border. The convoy normally took a few hours to complete the trip because of the mandated convoy speed limit of 20 miles per hour.[172]

The 1st and 3rd Brigades of the 25th Infantry Division normally provided road security along the Main Supply Route, but the Division's new Commander, Major General Ellis W. Williamson, had ordered the 3rd Brigade to Saigon. Convoy security was a high priority, but MACV respected the local commander's decision. The reduction in force resulted from the anticipated third phase of the Tet Offensive. From 17 to 24 August, the 1st Brigade had fought off 13 enemy battalion or regimental attacks, including seven attacks on the 1st Brigade's bases. The 1st Brigade's Intelligence Officer had determined that 16,000 combat-ready troops of the 5th and 9th NVA Divisions accompanied by an anti-aircraft battalion and two attached VC battalions would mass against it. The division's intelligence officer, however, believed Saigon was the main target. General Williamson then moved the 2nd Battalion, 34th Armor back to Cu Chi, while still ordering the 1st Brigade to secure the main supply route. This proved a fatal mistake. The brigade

[170] Rick Smith interview.
[171] Stephen C. Tunnell, "Convoy Ambush at Ap Nhi," *Vietnam*, April 1999.
[172] Ibid.

commander, Colonel Duquesne "Duke" Wolf, doubted whether he could defend his six bases, let alone the main supply route with his meager force. His brigade only had three undermanned rifle companies, three undermanned mechanized infantry companies, two 105mm artillery batteries, and two medium batteries with no armored cavalry units attached. Wolf challenged General Williamson's decision, to no avail. Only eight MP gun jeeps provided security for the 81 vehicles in the convoy.[173]

The village of Ap Nhi and the Ben Cui Rubber Plantation, known locally as Little Rubber, flanked Route 22 for about a mile. The Ap Nhi side was mostly farm land while the Little Rubber side had rubber trees growing to 15 feet of the road. A drainage ditch and an earthen berm paralleled the road inside the trees. Elements of the 88th NVA Regiment had moved into the Little Rubber the evening of 24 August to prepare an ambush. At 1145 hours the convoy entered the quiet village of Ap Nhi. It was misting and raining and the ceiling hung about 200 feet above the ground. The convoy passed what looked like a column of Army of the Republic of Vietnam (ARVN) soldiers marching along the north side of the road adjacent to the Little Rubber. The lead vehicles of the convoy had started to leave the village and the ammo and fuel vehicle were alongside the column when the supposed ARVN soldiers opened fire on the convoy. The soldiers turned out to be Viet Cong.[174]

This signaled the VC and NVA troops positioned in the Little Rubber to initiate an intense barrage of rocket, machinegun, and automatic-weapons fire on the convoy. The enemy first targeted the eight gun jeeps. The enemy then fired at the lead fuel trucks hoping to block part of the convoy. Two fuel tankers began to burn. 30 trucks in front of them sped away, following SOP, leaving 51 trucks stranded in the mile-long kill zone. The enemy then set two ammunition trailers of 105mm rounds on fire at the rear of the convoy sealing the trucks in place. The drivers climbed out of their vehicles and took up defensive positions either behind their trucks or in the ditch along the road. The enemy had thoroughly planned the ambush. It occurred well beyond the range of the 1st Brigade's artillery. Likewise, the low ceiling initially prevented the use of air support. With the convoy trapped, the enemy left their cover and made a rush on the column of trucks.[175]

When the convoy stopped, Specialist 4 William W. Seay, of the 62nd Transportation Company, immediately jumped out of his truck and took a defensive position behind the left rear dual wheels of his truck. Seay's trailer carried high-explosive artillery powder charges. Specialist 4 David M. Sellman, also of the 62nd, in the truck behind Seay did the same. Another driver joined him. The three drivers fought about 20 feet apart. When the North Vietnamese assault reached to within 10 meters of the road, Seay, who was the closest, opened fire, killing two of the enemy. Sellman shot one enemy soldier just 15 meters in front of him, then his M-16 jammed. The drivers, however, had successfully turned back the first enemy assault.[176]

---

173 Ibid.
174 Ibid.
175 Ibid.
176 Ibid.

The beleaguered drivers came under automatic fire from the berm and sniper fire from the trees. Seay spotted a sniper in a tree approximately 75 meters to his right front and killed him. Within minutes an enemy grenade rolled under the trailer within a few feet of Sellman. Without hesitation, Seay ran from his covered position while under intense enemy fire, picked up the grenade and threw it back to the North Vietnamese position. Four enemy soldiers jumped up from their covered position and tried to run when the grenade explosion killed them. Minutes later another enemy grenade rolled near the group of drivers. Sellman kicked it off the road behind him. After it exploded, another enemy grenade rolled under Seay's trailer approximately three meters from his position. Again Seay left his covered position and threw the armed grenade back at the enemy. At the same time Sellman shot an enemy soldier crawling through the fence. After returning to his position, Seay and Sellman killed two more NVA soldiers trying to crawl through the fence. Suddenly a bullet shattered the bone in Seay's right wrist. Seay called for Sellman to cover him as he ran back to the rear looking for someone to treat his wound.[177]

Seay located Lieutenant Howard Brockbank, Specialist 4 William Hinote, and four other drivers in a group. Hinote saw that Seay had lost much blood and was in pain. One man applied a sterile dressing on the wound, but it did not stop the bleeding. Hinote then tied a tourniquet around Seay's wrist with his shirt. Seay continued to give encouragement and direction to his fellow soldiers. Hinote mentioned his concern about Seay's shattered wrist. Seay told him to stay alive and not to worry about him. One soldier fired a full clip of his M-16 in one burst and Seay admonished him, "Take it easy! Don't waste your ammo—we may run out. What will we do then, stand up and fight them with our fists? I wouldn't be any good at that!"[178]

Weak from the loss of blood, Seay moved to the relative cover of a shallow ditch to rest. After another half hour of fighting, Hinote brought him some water. They occasionally fired at enemy positions while waiting for the next attack. Seay noticed three enemy soldiers who had crossed the road and were preparing to fire on his comrades. Seay raised to a half crouch and fired his rifle with his left hand, killing all three. Suddenly, a sniper's bullet struck Seay in the head, killing him instantly. He only had 60 days left in country.[179]

Two Huey UH-1C Model helicopters, equipped with two door gunners, 14 rockets, and a mini-gun, from Company B, 25th Aviation Battalion, responded first. Warrant Offier Robert J. "Bob" Spliter was one of the first to arrive. The commander on the ground informed him that the enemy was in the rubber plantation bordering the road. Spliter recognized drivers in the ditch and enemy soldiers unloading the American trucks. They carried the supplies into the tree line where they were loaded onto their own trucks. The gun ships had a tough time engaging the enemy. The low ceiling prevented the helicopters from attacking at regular angles. The Hueys normally rolled in on the target

[177] Ibid.
[178] Ibid.
[179] Ibid.

from a steep dive from about 1,500 feet. The pilots instead had to fly in above the tree tops and fire their rockets on a flat trajectory at point-blank range, all the while receiving enemy ground fire. After expending most of their fuel and ammunition, they hovered low over the tree line to save fuel and fired rockets, door guns and mini-guns at the enemy all simultaneously. The enemy was everywhere. Soon, the pilots ran out of ammunition and called for the next "Diamondhead" light-fire team to replace them. Spliter briefed them in the air and the transition of battle went seamlessly. The two helicopters flew back to Cu Chi to refuel, rearm, and wait for the next mission. Those helicopters helped hold the enemy at bay.[180]

The delay in the response of the 1st Brigade resulted from a communications problem and the remoteness of the ambush location. By 1430, tanks and infantry arrived in the area and 30 minutes later helicopters inserted two infantry companies. However, the burning fuel tankers blocked the road preventing tanks from advancing further to the aid of the drivers. Heavy enemy fire pinned the infantry down.[181]

A squad from the 65th Engineer Battalion, led by Sergeant Gregory Haley and accompanied by two APCs from the 1st Battalion, 5th Infantry, happened to be sweeping the road for mines and came upon the rear of the convoy. The APCs could not drive past the burning ammunition trailers and intense enemy fire. One of the .50 caliber machineguns on their APC was burned out from previous fighting and the other jammed continually. The squad engaged the enemy with M-60s, M-16s, and grenades. As ammunition began to run low, Sergeant Haley maneuvered to the rear of one of the APCs and secured more ammunition and another M-60. He jumped down from the APC only to realize his weapon had no trigger. He returned and grabbed another, fed a belt of ammunition into the M-60, and opened fire. The weapon jammed. He pulled the charging handle and it broke off in his hand.[182]

The battle continued for a couple more hours. Five tractors and a gun jeep, that had reached Tay Ninh, dropped their trailers and returned by a back road to help recover damaged vehicles and trailers. By then, the American infantry gained control of the kill zone. Around 2100, an armored cavalry troop finally arrived at the rear of the column and forced the enemy to withdraw. Seven drivers lost their lives in the ambush, 10 more were wounded and two were taken prisoner. The relief force lost 23 killed and 35 wounded. This was the first large scale ambush for the 48th Group.[183]

Lessons

This was the first major convoy ambush of the 48th Group in the III Corps Tactical Zone. The 48th Group relied entirely on the combat arms units for protection. As COL Paul Swanson learned, this external support was subject to the decision of the combat arms commander based on competing priorities. The arbitrary decision of the area commander to defend Saigon stripped the area of combat arms support and required the reaction force

[180] Leonard, Ron, "The Ambush At Ap Nhi," unpublished.
[181] Tunnell, "Ambush at Ap Nhi."
[182] Ibid.
[183] Ibid.

to come from a greater distance. In the absence of gun trucks or combat arms, the drivers had to fight as infantry men. They needed to know all the skills for setting up a defense and coordinating fire support.

Action

Having faced a devastating convoy ambush similar to what 8th Group experienced on 2 September, the 48th Transportation Group came up with a different solution to ambushes than the 8th Group. The 48th Group started by making everyone wear their helmets and protective vests. The two truck battalions had not had anyone killed in an ambush since 22 November 1966 and the drivers had become complacent and quit wearing protective gear because of the heat. The 48th Group also required that trucks include assistant drivers or "shotguns" to ride along. This added extra riflemen in a fight. In previous ambushes, they had followed the SOP to not stop in the kill zone, but they had no choice if vehicles blocked the narrow roads as on 25 August. They could not turn around and drive out of the kill zone. In this case, the drivers had to fight as infantry until the nearest reaction force arrived. The slow response by the reaction force on 25 August was an embarrassment for the 25th Infantry Division, so the Soldiers set out to resolve the problem.[184]

In August 1968, representatives from the MP, division, and transportation units held several conferences to define relationships. According to a report in 1971, the Provost Marshal of the 25th Infantry Division assumed responsibility for convoy security for the 48th Group convoys. He flew overhead in an aircraft and shared control of the convoy with the convoy commander on the ground. In the event of an ambush, infantry or cavalry commanders assumed control of the convoy.[185]

Colonel Paul Swanson assumed command of the 48th Group in November 1968. Swanson opposed the use of gun trucks. This is surprising since the 48th Group had previously built armored gun trucks. In the fall of 1967, the 6th Battalion received the tasking to conduct a night convoy south to support the 9th Infantry Division. Anticipating ambushes, the 6th Battalion welded steel plates to the doors of 20 light trucks and two jeeps. They also fabricated a machinegun mount and welded it to the right side of the cab so that the assistant driver could fire the machinegun while standing up. The convoy was ambushed and the trucks repelled the attackers. The battalion conducted no more night convoys and the idea of gun trucks did not spread any further in the 48th Group.[186]

Instead, Swanson believed the combat commander had the responsibility for convoy security. The ambushes usually ended when the infantry and tanks arrived and swept through the area. He did not want to crowd into the infantry's mission or take task vehicles off the road. Swanson did, however, allow drivers to put steel plating on the sides of their cabs for individual protection. The main issue with the ambush at Ap Nhi was that the field commander arbitrarily pulled the infantry from defending the road to

---

[184] BG Orvil C. Metheny Interview by CPT Louis C. Johnson, 22 November 1985 and BG (R) Orvil Metheny summary of telephone interview by Richard Killblane, 19 March 2004.
[185] Metheny interviews and Thomas, Vehicle Convoy Security," p. II-32.
[186] Discussion with LTC (R) Larry Ondic.

defending Saigon leaving the convoys vulnerable. The trucks needed some guarantee the combat arms would not leave them unprotected again. Swanson told the 1st and 25th Infantry Divisions that if they wanted their cargo to pass through, they needed to keep the enemy off of his convoys. It helped that the G3 of the 25th Infantry Division was a classmate of his from the Army War College. For the next year, the 25th Infantry Division provided excellent support. This relationship was all personality-driven though.[187]

[187] Metheny interviews.

Operation Iraqi Freedom

23 March 2003, An Nasariyah
507th Maintenance Company
See Executive Summary

Lesson
This attack on the 507th Maintenance Company would at best be classified as a hasty ambush resulting in the loss of 11 Soldiers killed seven captured and nine wounded. There were a number of mistakes made but the Soldiers and leaders performed as they were trained. This attack sent shock waves through the combat service support units by reminding them that there was no longer a safe rear. What the Soldiers and leaders assigned to the truck units failed to learn from this ambush, the Vietnam veterans did. Immediately after this ambush hit the news, Vietnam veterans called the Transportation Corps Historian telling him that gun trucks would have prevented or reduced the loss of life. This attack was a warning and few recognized it.

Our enemy's study our history to determine how to defeat us. Most do not go back any further than the Vietnam War. The main lesson our adversaries learn is that the best way to defeat the American Army is to inflict casualties. Our media focuses on the loss of life to a point that overshadows any victories on the ground. Of all the heroic battles on the ground, the media focused more on the prisoners from the 507th elevating Jessica Lynch to hero status. Little attention was paid to SPC Miller of that company whose heroic actions during that ambush earned him the Silver Star Medal. This focus on loss versus gain by the American media was not lost on the enemy. All they had to do to make the Americans go home was kick up the body count.

June 2003
Tiger Team/Convoy Rat Patrol
From the beginning of Operation Iraqi Freedom in March 2003, the MPs had the responsibility to escort convoys. Combined Forces Land Component Command (CFLCC) required two HMMVs to escort a convoy regardless of its size. The problem was most of them were unarmored and armed with nothing more than an M-249 SAW. The convoys they escorted had more fire power than that. At first, the attacks mostly targeted individual trucks with small arms, RPGs and IEDs along MSR Tampa. The shortage of MP escorts and the increased threat to convoys in Iraq beginning in May 2003 inspired the rebirth of the gun truck.

Some officers believed that gun trucks would not have any effect on this level of threat. In war, tactics, techniques and procedures (TTP) are always evolving. As the TTPs on one side evolve, the TTPs of the other reciprocate. In tactics, nothing remains constant, yet some of those responsible for doctrine and technology saw each step as an end rather than a progression. Not only that but the normal process for research, development, test and procurement is painfully slow. While those responsible for doctrine and technology debated over the appropriate solution, the truck drivers and mechanic took maters in their own hands. The threat was real to them and they saw the gun truck as an immediate solution to their problem. Once again, the development of the gun truck was a Transportation Corps initiative.

The initial threat in the summer of 2003 challenged the 181st Transportation Battalion at Anaconda, which had responsibility for the convoys along MSR Tampa. In June, the insurgents killed a civilian contract driver of Kellogg, Brown and Root (KBR) and the rest refused to drive into Iraq without military escort. The battalion commander, LTC Chuck Maskell, tasked CPT Isaac Bristow, commander of the 2632nd Transportation Company, to build 30 gun trucks to provide command and control over the civilian convoys. Again the issue came down to armor and armament. There already was an M-1114 armored HMMV with a ring mount in the inventory, but not enough to meet the demands of convoys in Iraq. Not until early 2005, would the commercial industry produce enough M-1114s or add-on armor kits to fulfill the increased demands of the war.

Instead mechanics welded sheet metal to the sides of M998 HMMVs and because the soft tops could not support ring mounts, they constructed gun boxes on the backs of HMMVs. The welders of the 181st Battalion experimented with gun truck designs in a section of the maintenance area known as the "Skunk Werks." As the ambush threat spread to other areas later that year, so did the development of HMMV gun truck designs. There was a wide variety of designs, some good and some bad. This led to the term "hillbilly armor." Because the cabs of the HMMVs did not have ring mounts or support the weight of a ring mount, the HMMV designs primarily consisted of an armored box and mounted the machinegun in the back. Machinegun mounts were either pedestal, ring mount welded on a box or swivel seat. Some HMMV gun trucks even mounted machineguns on swivel arms hinged to the back doors like helicopter door guns. Any vehicle with an M-249 (SAW) was considered a gun truck.

This is where history rhymed. The Vietnam gun jeep could not support the weight of full armor protection as the 5-ton gun truck. However, since the HMMV was designed to replace both the jeep and the 2 ½-ton truck, the HMMV gun truck combined the best attributes of both in terms of armor and armament. Although it could maneuver like a gun jeep it did not carry the number of crew served weapons as the gun truck. There was still the need for bigger gun trucks.

The larger gun truck designs either consisted of a machinegun mounted on a ring mount over the cab or for those vehicles that could not fit a ring mount, the crews constructed a sandbag and plywood box on the back of the 5-ton truck. Many built roofs over their gun boxes to provide shade from the sun, thus giving the appearance of a "dog house." It did not take long to figure out that sandbags fell apart with the beating of the rough road. Crews began to experiment with steel walls. Remarkably some would find their inspiration for gun trucks from photos of Vietnam gun trucks on the internet. Their only limitation was the availability of steel. They had taken the same first step as the 8th Group had in Vietnam.

Inspired by Dean Dominique's article, "Convoy Rat Patrol," CPT Bristow developed a doctrine around the HMMV gun trucks he called "Tiger Teams." Two HMMV gun trucks ran almost a kilometer ahead of convoys to block traffic at intersections so the convoys could pass without slowing down or stopping. In the event of an ambush, they would respond to the threat with fire power. Other units adopted this doctrine. The Tiger Teams attempted to replace the role of both the gun jeeps and gun trucks of Vietnam. The dog house and ring mounts gun trucks just maintained their positions in the convoy. The idea spread to other units in Iraq and they returned the name to "Rat Patrols."

The private military contractor, Military Professional Resources Inc. (MPRI), also took the initiative to develop a convoy live fire training program at Camp Udari, Kuwait. JTF7 saw the need to send units back to Kuwait for this training. MPRI began by teaching the drivers to dismount their vehicles and fight when in the kill zone. Taking feedback from drivers, MPRI continually evolved their training. They quickly changed the ambush doctrine to clear the kill zone. One of their most significant contributions was the concept of the floating rally point, where convoys would form a box a couple miles beyond the kill zone. As gun trucks evolved, so did the MPRI training program making them the proponent for convoy ambush battle drills.

OIF2

Inspiration of the turn, fix and fire tactic

While the following study does not focus on one ambush, it provides a little background on an officer who would play a prominent role in the development of the tactic, techniques and procedures (TTP) of the 518th Gun Truck Company. After the April Uprising, both Multi-national Corps-Iraq (MNCI) in Iraq and Combined Force Land Component Command (CFLCC) in Kuwait would direct the creation of gun truck companies. Although there was an effort from higher command to standardize TTPs, each gun truck unit would develop their own.

This also illustrates one of the problems with unit rotation. The official policy in OIF has been to rotate units upon completion of one-year boots on the ground (BOG). The problem is that within a few months, the Army has all new units fighting the war. They have a short right seat/left seat ride period before the transfer of authority, then the new units have to learn how to fight the war all over. Each year the Iraqi insurgents gain more experience fighting the Americans, yet the American units on the ground only gain one year experience fighting the Iraqis then leave. The replacement of OIF 1 units was pretty much completed by March 2004.

The 1487th Transportation Company, National Guard from Eaton, Ohio, arrived in Kuwait on 3 February 2004. It was sent Cedar II and conducted its right-seat-ride with the 740th Medium Truck Company, from South Dakota, in February. The 740th had conducted Sustainer Push from Kuwait to Cedar II and had never been hit during its year tour. The 1487th Transportation Company's first right seat ride with the 740th was a five to seven-day trip to the Syrian border.[188]

---

[188] 1LT James L. McCormick II, "The 518th Combat Gun Truck Company (Provisional) 'U.S. Regulators,'" *Transportation Corps Professional Bulletin*, Winter 2004.

1LT James McCormick II was a platoon leader in the 1487th TC at Navistar. He had been a squad leader in a scout platoon during Operation Desert Storm. His convoy departed Cedar II for BIAP. They RONed at BIAP and departed the next morning at 0600. A pair of Apache helicopter gun ships escorted the convoy on ASR Mobile when an IED exploded next to an M-915. The explosion damaged the truck and wounded both drivers. SPC Jacob Bach became the first Soldier of the 1487th to become wounded in action.[189]

McCormick asked the platoon leader, "What next?" She looked at him and said that this had never happened to her convoy before. Most of the problems occurred north of CSC Scania and the 740th usually just ran convoys to Cedar II near An Nasariyah and back. This was also their first run beyond Cedar. The platoon leader pulled out her folder with the radio frequencies and medevac procedures. McCormick was surprised that no one had memorized the frequencies but him. They called for the medevac but since the helicopter had been shot down near Fallujah, they told the convoy to bring the wounded in. When McCormick walked back to the damaged truck, he saw Soldiers milling around and taking pictures as if it was a traffic accident. They were still in the kill zone. He yelled at the drivers to get back in their trucks. They continued to Camp Champion near Al Ramadi and finished the six-day run without further incident.[190]

After that convoy, McCormick's crew painted alternating tan and black stripes on the shell of his HMMV. This made it very noticeable. McCormick wanted to name it something more fitting of its offensive role, like "the Striped Avenger" or "the Raptor," but SPC Thomas Selemi jokingly called it, "the Zebra." McCormick remembered that zebras run. He asked, "Have you ever seen a zebra turn and fight?" The rest of the crew thought the name was funny. They reminded him that it looked like a zebra, so he let them call it that. Attracting attention is good unless one is good at what he does. McCormick and his HMMV crew would have plenty of opportunity to prove themselves. His platoon also added a ring mount to the top of an M-915 5-ton and constructed a steel gun box on the back.[191]

On 22 March, the 1487th escorted a 70 plus convoy north. An IED exploded next to an M-915 just past the second bridge on ASR Mobile. McCormick turned the Zebra and the M-915 gun truck back to secure the damaged vehicle. It received fire from two insurgents maneuvering behind a small building. The Zebra did not have any crew served weapons, so the crew dismounted and laid down suppressive fire with their M-16s and SAWs. The 5-ton made four passes firing its M-60 machinegun. In ten minutes of fighting, the Americans killed the two insurgents.[192]

April Uprising

---

[189] McCormick, "518th Gun Truck."
[190] McCormick, "518th Gun Truck."
[191] McCormick, "518th Gun Truck," and telephone interview with McCormick by Richard Killblane, 23 July 2005.
[192] McCormick email and "518th Gun Truck."

On 31 March, four civilian contract body guards of the Blackwater Security Consulting, which provided security for food deliveries, drove into Fallujah and their vehicle was attacked. The contactors were killed, their bodies mutilated beyond recognition, burned and what was left was hung on the bridge over the Euphrates. BG Mark Kimmitt, Deputy Director for Coalition Operations, pledged to hunt down those who carried out killings, but added that he would not send forces into Fallujah to retrieve the remains of the victims. He asked the Iraqi police to recover the remains. Kimmit feared that any coalition forces entering the city would encounter ambushes where the insurgents would use civilians as human shields and any pre-emptive attack into the city could lead to a bad situation and make it even worse. The US military would instead act on the time and place of its choosing. This hesitancy seemed to encourage the insurgents. Violence spread to other regions in the Suni Triangle.

At 1300 hours on Tuesday, 5 April 2005, the Mosques in the Suni Triangle called for Iraqi people to take up arms in a jihad against the coalition forces. A car bomb exploded next to a patrol of three US armored vehicles and two HMMVs in Al Ramadi at 1700 hours, that day.

A platoon from the 1486th Medium Truck stationed at Cedar II escorted a KBR Class IX Sustainer Push convoy to LSA Anaconda. On 5 April, SSG Dan Studer's squad escorted a KBR convoy returning from Anaconda. At 0745, three insurgents fired small arms and an RPG from a dump truck. The convoy continued to move and did not return fire. At 0750 on ASR Sword, the same convoy received more small arms fire bowing out the rear duals on a KBR truck. The convoy continued to a rally point without returning fire. At the rally point, the KBR truck changed its tires. At 0905, an orange and white vehicle approached from the rear at a high rate of speed and two passengers fired at the convoy. The convoy returned fire and injured on of the insurgents. SGT Hubert applied first aid until a medevac arrived. At 1130, a taxi with five insurgents fired on the convoy. Upon reaching CSC Scania, KBR pulled their convoys off of the road. The squad returned to Cedar. The convoy had been ambushed four times in four hours.[193]

On 6 April, a fuel convoy of the 724th POL escorted a KBR convoy from Anaconda through the town of Hit. As CPT Terrence Henry's lead vehicle drove through the traffic circle on ASR Bronze, the SAW gunner, SPC Russell, noticed the absence of ICDC in the circle. As he turned to look back, he saw Iraqi gunmen come out from behind cars just as an IED exploded on the right side of the road. They had detonated it too early and it missed the trucks. Russell fired off 13 rounds at the insurgents as they opened fire. SGT Bailey and SGT Watson in the approaching 5-ton gun truck saw the exchange of gun fire and also engaged targets with their Mk-19 grenade launcher. SGT Bailey began picking off insurgents hiding in the doorways and behind cars. The 724th POL had its first ambush and suffered no casualties or had any trucks damaged.[194]

[193] "1486th Transportation Company Easter Week Firefights."

[194] SSG Paul L. Marsh and SSG Victor L. Febus, "On the Move with the 724th Transportation Company: Patriots in the Middle East," n.d., and "Historical Narrative, 724th Transportation Company," n.d.

On 7 April, IEDs closed the southbound traffic. The Muqtada al Sadr's al Mahdi Army clashed with elements of the 1st Cavalry Division and attacked a convoy on ASR Cardinals. The next day, Mahdi Army attacked convoys and clashed with elements of the 1st Cavalry Division and 1st Armored Division on ASR Sword and Cardinals.[195]

As the violence flared up, the insurgents blew up several bridges over the Euprhates River to severe the line of communication in their area. While this actually hurt their own citizens more, guerrillas often tend to blow up bridges to hinder the government civic action and make them appear helpless in the eyes of the people they are trying to win. The movement controller rerouted traffic while the Army engineers quickly spanned the bridges.

Since 7 April, the 2/12th Cavalry, based out of Camp Victory at BIAP, fought with the Mahdi militia to reassert control over their area of operations. The Cavalry patrols were frequently attacked by insurgents on ASR Sword and Cardinals. The buildings along the streets provided excellent concealment for the insurgents to fire down upon the passing vehicles. Some insurgents felt so bold as to drive right up to the tanks and Bradleys and fire RPGs at them. At 0300 in the morning of 9 April, CPT Munz ordered his patrol of C, 2/12 Cav to take the Dairy Milk Factory from which the insurgents had launched their attacks. The Cavalry patrol settled in to a defensive perimeter for the rest of the morning.[196]

Good Friday, 9 April 2005
Ambush at Abu Ghraib
724th Transportation Company (POL), 7th Transportation Battalion

On 8 April, the 724th Transportation Company (POL) was tasked to escort KBR drivers on an emergency fuel push from Logistic Support Area Anaconda to Camp Webster, near Al Asad, the next morning. This US Army Reserve fuel tanker company was from Bartonville, Illinois. 1LT Matthew "Matt" Brown, of the 2nd Platoon, would lead the convoy. 9 April was Good Friday and coincidently the first anniversary of the fall of Baghdad. For an enemy that liked to attack on significant dates or anniversaries, this weekend had plenty of significance.[197]

At 2330 hours their destination changed to BIAP. The company commander, CPT Jeffrey Smith, went to battalion operations to find out what was going on. The new route was ASR Milton, MSR Tampa, ASR Vernon to ASR Irish arriving at Entry Control Point (ECP) 1. Since no one in the company had driven to BIAP, except when they passed through there on their way to Anaconda in March, he requested a right-seat rider guide. SFC Hawley, of the 1742nd Transportation Company, was tasked to meet them in the staging area at 0700 hours the next morning. CPT Smith also asked for air coverage along the route and the battalion forwarded the request.[198]

---

[195] Power Point, "April 9th Ambush,"

[196] SSG Paul L. March, "On the move with the 724th Transportation Company: Patriots in the Middle East," unpublished.

[197] CPT Jeffry Smith, "Historical Narrative; 724th Transportation Company," unpublished.

[198] Smith, "Narrative."

The 724th also had a requirement to provide "shooters" to ride shotgun with the KBR drivers. Kellogg, Brown and Root (KBR) would provide the drivers for the "green" military fuel trucks and the 724th would provide the gun trucks and right seat-riders. This was also their first time to provide right seat riders for KBR.[199]

KBR had the contract for transporting fuel. Since the insurgents had killed the first contract driver in June 2003, these unarmed civilian truckers required an armed military escort. The 724th Transportation Company had inherited the mission. KBR provided their drivers with brand new Mercedes trucks, but for this convoy they would drive military tractors.

At 0500 on 9 April, 1LT Brown reported to the battalion TOC for the intelligence briefing on the route. Thomas Hamill, the convoy commander for the KBR drivers, reported for his security briefing at 0600 hours. The KBR security advisor told him that all routes were red, which meant that they could not drive. He said he would check with the military and check if the roads were still closed.[200]

CJTF7 employed four colors to classify threat levels on any route. Black referred to imminent or ongoing enemy contact, and the route should be avoided if at all possible. Red warned of the existence of a serious threat. Amber indicated some threat exists, or that enemy contact had occurred on that route within the last 24 hours. Green indicated little to no threat.

Hamill then reported to the Total Safety Task Instruction (TSTI) with the rest of the drivers to learn who was going out with him that day. He then gathered the 19 other drivers assigned to his convoy to talk about the road conditions. About that time, the security advisor walked up and informed him that the routes had been cleared and route status changed to amber. Hamill sensed that the security advisor was still apprehensive. Of the 19 "green" military tractors, 17 hauled 5,000 gallon tankers and two were bob tails, to pick up any systems in case of a break down. After the meeting, the contract drivers climbed into their tractors and fired up the engines.[201]

The 724th escort vehicles left their motor pool to link up with the KBR drivers. Although the Corps policy required a ratio of 1:10 escort vehicles to prime movers, that day the 724th ran with five gun trucks; two M998s (HMMV), two M931s (5-ton tractor) and one M923 (5-ton cargo). At that time, any vehicle with a crew-served weapon, such as an M-249 SAW or Mk-19 grenade launcher, was considered a gun truck. There was no requirement for armor. One M915 tractor carried a Warlock jamming system. A M998 from the 644th TC accompanied the convoy for a total of 26 vehicles. That reduced the gun truck ratio to 1:4.[202]

---

199 Smith "Narrative."

200 Thomas Hamill and Paul T. Brown, *Escape in Iraq; The Thomas Hamill Story*, Accokeek, Maryland: Stoeger Publishing Company, 2004.

201 Hamill, *Escape in Iraq*.

202 Thomas Hamill and Paul T. Brown, *Escape In Iraq; The Thomas Hamill Story*, Accokeck, MD: Stoeger Publishing Company, 2004.

1LT Brown gave the convoy brief then SFC Hawley briefed the route. That is when the KBR drivers learned that they were driving to BIAP instead of Camp Webster. The KBR foreman had to run back to run back to his Transportation Operations to submit a new mission sheet. Meanwhile, SFC Tolson walked up and informed them that Battalion had called on the SINCGARS radio and changed the last part of the route to ASR Sword and Cardinal entering at ECP 4, the North Gate at BIAP. CPT Smith, 1LT Brown and SFC Hawley walked over to their HMMV to call Battalion and verify the route change. Hawley asked for and received the exit number to ASR Cardinal. He then briefed the new route and drew the route out in the sand and gravel of the staging area. He mentioned that he had only made one trip to the North Gate but was sure he could do it again. The entire route should take about two hours.[203]

At 0957, just 30 minutes prior to Brown's SP time, the Chief of Highway Operations for the 172nd General Support Group rerouted the convoy to BIAP's northern gate because of a suspected IED was discovered along the ASR Irish at Check Point 1. The movement control battalion listed their route as red, enemy contact likely. When the Chief finally contacted the 2/12th Cavalry battle captain, the captain informed the Chief that ASR Cardinals had been closed for three days due to intense fighting. Just the day before, the Mahadi Army had attacked convoys and clashed with the 1st Cavalry in the same area the 724th POL had to drive. The Chief then sent another email message intended for the 49th Movement Control Battalion, "Sorry, it looks like Sword is closed until further notice. I am trying to deconflict." The MCB never received the message. The Chief later learned that he accidentally emailed the message to himself.[204]

The first serial, which was escorted by the 2632nd Air Expeditionary Force (USAF) rolled out the gate at 1000 hours but had problems with its SINCGARS and turned back. As the first serial returned, the rest of the 724th escort arrived and Brown gave another convoy briefing. He told the drivers that they would head southwest out the gate to MSR Tampa, then proceed south through Taji to ASR Sword where the convoy would turn west for then after two miles turn south and drive right into BIAP.[205]

1LT Brown had a total of 23 Soldiers, six of which were assigned as shooters for the KBR drivers. Hamill assigned a shooter to every other truck. The Battalion XO, MAJ Pagent, was at the staging area and made the call to send out Brown's convoy serial first since it was ready. They hit the front gate at 1030 hours. Meanwhile, the 2632nd convoy resolved its problem and departed at 1055 hours as the second serial.[206]

The 724th convoy drove out the gate onto a six-lane highway. PFC Jeremy Church drove the convoy commander's HMMV at the head of the convoy with SFC Hawley as the route guide and SGT Blankenship as the SAW gunner. SPC Adams and 1LT Howard, from the 644th Transportation Company, rode in the second HMMV. Hamill followed in

---

203 Smith, "Narrative," and Hamill, *Escape*.
204 March, "On the move."
205 Smith, "Narrative" and Hamill, *Escape*.
206 Smith, "Narrative" and Hamill, *Escape*.

the tractor driven by Nelson Howell. The next 5-ton gun truck with SPC Row and SPC McDermott on the M2 .50 caliber followed behind four KBR trucks. SSG Grage drove for SPC Brown, five KBR vehicles behind. SGT Watson manned the Mk-19 of SPC Bachman's gun truck behind Grage. Five more KBR trucks followed with SPC Lamar driving a HMMV with SFC Groff, as the assistant convoy commander, and SPC Pelz as the SAW gunner. Five more vehicles behind that SPC Kirkpatrick drove the last gun truck with SPC Bohm manning the M2. Essentially, there was one crew served weapon between every four to five task vehicles.[207]

More often, problems with the vehicles or drivers occur early on. Hamill had three new drivers assigned to his convoy from another department that morning. He saw in his rear view mirror that two of them were having problems keeping the proper 100 meter interval between trucks. One kept falling back. He coached the new driver with his radio every few minutes and by the time they turned south onto Tampa, the spacing was correct.[208]

The first part of the drive was uneventful, but after an hour and a half of driving, Iraqi vehicles started swerved off the side of the road and the convoy drivers saw fewer and fewer locals, a clear indication of trouble ahead. At 1230 hours, the convoy turned onto ASR Sword, a stretch of road known as "IED Alley." The trucks had to dodge rocks and tires in the road intended to slow them down. There were buildings on both sides of the road.

Tommy Zimmerman, in the fourth vehicle in the convoy, radioed Hamill that his truck was dying on him. The standard procedure was to have gun truck come up to the disabled vehicle and pull security until a bobtail could hook up and tow the whole tractor and trailer system off. Hamill radioed 1LT Brown "I've got a truck that is breaking down. We need to get gun support there with him." Suddenly one of the bob tails in the rear reported that it was taking gun fire. Hamill urged Brown, "We need to get this man picked up. Get the gun truck to pick him up. Let's leave the truck, just get the men." At that moment, Brown and Hamill had little idea how bad the situation had turned behind them.[209]

SGT Watson, in the 15th vehicle in line of march, noticed that civilian cars stopped on the right side of the road then backed up. Soon after, he heard a large explosion and saw a fuel truck ahead of him, possibly the 7th or 11th vehicle in line of march, explode. As he entered the kill zone, Watson received small arms fire from the left side of the road. He immediately returned fire with his Mk-19, but the black smoke prevented him from seeing the enemy.[210]

Suddenly, everyone reported on their radios receiving enemy fire. The enemy initiated the ambush with small arms and RPGs fired from both sides of the road. In the past, the

[207] March, "On the move."
[208] Hamill, *Escape*.
[209] Hamill, *Escape*.
[210] March, "On the move."

length of kill zones had been very short, not more than a few hundred meters at most. The common response was to "put peddle to the metal" and drive through as fast as one could, which was about 45 miles per hour towing a 5,000 gallon load of fuel. What they did not know was that they had entered a four to five mile kill zone laid by 150 to 200 of Sadr's black-clad militia. Burning fuel trucks along the road would create a scene imagined only in hell and the wind blew the smoke across their path blinding the drivers and crews. The drive through the hail of gun and rocket fire seemed endless.

PFC Jarob Walsh, 19th in line of march, heard 1LT Brown on the radio, "We are taking rounds - everyone get ready!" Then not even a minute later, someone else incorrectly reported, "The LT's truck just blew up and I don't know where to go or what to do!" Walsh looked at his driver, Raymond Stannard, and said "Oh shit it's about to get bad." He saw a smoking truck, what he thought was the 11th in line of march driven by Tony Johnson, with PFC Maupin as the shooter, lose power and drop back to a hundred meters in front of his then explode into a ball of flames. It swerved off the right side of the road, through the ditch and into buildings.[211]

SFC Groff driving the armored HMMV gun truck, 21st in line of march, saw the burning tanker on the right side of the road and the wind blew the smoke across the road. As soon as he passed the burning tanker, he received small arms fire from both sides of the road.[212]

With rounds now pummeling his HMMV, 1LT Brown reported back to the other trucks, "There's a truck on fire up ahead, we've gotta get off this road." The insurgents had set their own fuel tankers on fire. PFC Church turned off the highway through a hole cut in the guardrail. The trucks immediately behind him followed. Meanwhile, his gunner, SPC Blankenship, returned fire with the SAW.[213]

Hamill grabbed the Qualcomm on-board satellite computer and typed out a message warning the serial behind them, "Convoy under attack." Just then a bullet slammed through the door striking his forearm, knocking the computer out of his hands. The round blew a huge chunk of meat away, so he wrapped a clean sock around his arm to stop the bleeding. He then handed the radio to his driver, Nelson Howell. Just then, Hamill's truck began to have its own mechanical problems and slowed down. Other trucks began to speed past them on both the frontage road and highway.[214]

At the same time, Church drove aggressively to avoid the blast of IEDs and enemy emplaced obstacles, such as guardrails, concrete barriers, and vehicles, intended to slow down the convoy. Within the first five minutes of the ambush, two enemy rounds struck the convoy commander, 1LT Brown, wounding him in the head. While still driving, Church grabbed his first aid pouch, ripped it open and instructed 1LT Brown to place the bandage over his left eye. Church continued to fire his M16A2 out the window with one

---

[211] March, "On the move." Walsh's colleagues claim that he has a reputation for exaggeration.
[212] March, "On the move." Walsh's colleagues claim that he has a reputation for exaggeration.
[213] March, "On the move."
[214] Hamill, *Escape*.

hand while navigating through the obstacles all the while encouraging his platoon leader to prevent him from slipping into unconsciousness. He told 1LT Brown to close the ballistic window to prevent further injury just moments before another IED detonated on the front right side of the vehicle and blew out the front right tire. Continuing to fire his weapon with one hand, PFC Church kept his other hand on the steering wheel and pushed the vehicle ahead on three inflated tires.[215]

PFC Church finally reached the exit ramp, drove up on the overpass, turned left and drove down ASR Cardinal. He led what he could of the convoy to a security perimeter established by C/2-12 Cavalry the day before. All the while, enemy fire continued right up to the gates of the Dairy Milk Factory. Upon his arrival, Church described to the cavalry the ambush he had just driven. Church then carried his convoy commander to the casualty collection point for further treatment and medevac. The cavalry platoon leader assisted in medevacing the wounded drivers that had reached safety.[216]

Meanwhile, the remainder of the convoy bore the brunt of the enemy wrath. Small arms fire riddled the sides of the fuel tankers causing them to spill their contents on the road like water sprinklers making the road slippery. RPGs slammed into four tankers causing their liquid contents to explode into flames blanketing the road with thick black smoke. Some of the tractors still managed to drive with their loads on fire. The enemy had also detonated their own fuel trucks along side the road turning the road into a living hell.

An RPG hit the fuel truck driven by William Bradley, seventh in line of march. A heavy volume of small arms fire riddled the gun truck behind it, driven by Row, blowing out the mirrors. All the while, McDermott, eighth in line of march, blazed away with his .50 caliber machinegun as brass cartridges piled up at his feet. SPC Row simultaneously fired out the window with his M-16. As they reached the exit ramp to make the left turn onto the overpass, the burning fuel truck in front of them slid off of the road and flipped on its right side killing the driver. The smoke from the burning fuel swept across the road obscuring vision.[217]

The 13th truck driven by Jack Montague, with PFC Gregory R. Goodrich as his shooter, also came to a stop. SSG Grage's gun truck, 14th in line of march, came upon a fuel truck losing power. They pushed him for about a mile until they reached the overpass while SPC Brown returned fire. They could not push him any further. Grage's own vehicle took a beating. The radiator was overheating and one round went through the side window and out the front, the next round penetrated the left door and hit Grage in his left leg.[218]

---

[215]SPC Jeremy Church Silver Star Citation and March, "On the move."
[216] Church Citation.
[217] March, "On the move."
[218] March, "On the move."

As Hamill's truck slipped further back in the convoy, one tanker system a half a mile ahead of him began fishtailing on the slippery road then slid off onto the median, flipped over and exploded. The driver did not have a chance to escape.[219]

After passing Maupin's burning truck, Walsh, 19th in line of march, came upon the tanker flipped over on its side in the median. He then came upon another ahead on the right where he saw a man lying prone, raising his head up and down to watch them. Walsh propped his weapon on the side mirror of his truck and took aim for the man's head thinking he was an insurgent intending to blow up both trucks as they passed. He then saw that the man was holding something up something white in his left hand. Walsh's heart was pounding so hard, that he was sure it was a remote detonator, but he kept looking and held his fire. The closer they approached; Walsh recognized that the man was an American holding his ID card in an effort to let them know he was one of their KBR drivers. They could not stop to help.[220]

After they passed the civilian hiding behind the tanker, Walsh looked in his mirror and saw the truck behind him explode, roll over and slide down the highway. He had never seen anything like it before, "It really shook me up, it was just like something you would see in the movies." They then drove blindly through the smoke of five or six burning Iraqi tankers, with Walsh praying that they would not run into anything. The fire made it extremely hot and Walsh could hardly breathe with the smoke.[221]

Lester and Fisher brought up the rear in two bobtails. They looked for stranded drivers as they followed the path of destruction. Fisher picked up one soldier and a driver before being wounded himself. Lester rescued another driver, but heard one voice on the radio, screaming at him to come back, "Jack, you bastard, come back!," Lester had no idea where the man was or how to get to him, he said. "I could hear him saying. I couldn't handle that. I didn't want to answer. I didn't want to tell him, 'I can't help you.'" The situation had become a desperate live and death struggle for the drivers.[222]

After a while, Walsh and Stannard cleared the smoke and saw a truck in front of them traveling about twenty miles per hour with its trailer on fire. In an attempt to help, they slowed down. Walsh yelled at the driver telling him to stop and they would pick them up. It was Hamill and Nelson. Walsh's tractor pulled ahead of them a little. At that moment, Hamill's truck shook violently from the explosion of an RPG which also blew the other truck sideways. Walsh's driver luckily kept our tractor under control. Nelson yelled to Hamill, "We've been hit by something – some-thing big!" Hamill yelled, "We gotta keep going!"[223]

Further ahead Walsh recognized the overpass. One truck was already traveling over the bridge, and another was behind about a mile or two back with Groff's HMMV trailing

---

[219] Hamill, *Escape*.
[220] In his later testimony, Walsh mistakenly assumed that man was Tommy Hamill.
[221] Walsh.
[222] Christian Miller, IRAQ: Halliburton Convoy Unprepared for Last, Fatal Run," The Los Angeles Times March 26th, 2005 http://www.corpwatch.org/article.php?id=11999
[223] Walsh and Hamill, *Escape*.

behind it. Walsh's rig drove up the onramp, but as they turned left to towards BIAP, his driver started yelling. Walsh leaned forward and saw the smoke trail of an RPG heading toward his truck.[224]

Walsh later remembered, "The next thing I knew, our truck rolled onto its passenger side. I had my seat belt on so I couldn't move, but my driver didn't, and fell down on top of me, kicking and screaming trying to get out of the truck. He was all over me. I started hitting the windshield with the buttstock of my weapon until I broke through it. He ran out through it, turned around, and started pulling at my Kevlar helmet. He was trying to pull me out of the truck by my helmet, but my knee was stuck between the seat and dash, and my seatbelt was still on holding me back. He continued pulling on my helmet really hard, and at first I told him to get down and take cover, because we were still being fired at. But then it got to the point that I couldn't breathe. It felt like my head was going to pop, he was pulling so hard. Finally, I unstrapped my helmet and he fell backwards off me. I yelled at him and told him to get back in and lie down, but he was not listening, instead he came after me again. I unstrapped my seatbelt and pulled my knee out of the dash, falling down on my behind as my feet went out the window.[225]

"Next he started pulling my ankles to get me out of the truck. I kept yelling at him to get down but he wouldn't listen, so finally I kicked him in the chest with my left foot, and in the face with my right. As I kicked him in the face, he fell backwards. Before he hit the ground, blood splattered all over his face. I thought he had gotten shot, I thought 'd*** he's dead and now I'm alone.' But he fell back on his behind and just sat there. I thought, 'that's weird he's not dead.' I was sure he had been shot in the face, but then his eyes got big and he said, 'Oh my G** you've been shot, I'm going to die I'm going to die.' I looked down and didn't see any bullet holes. I had no idea what he was talking about. Then I looked at him and said, "Lay the f*** down and do not get up," just to keep him safe."[226]

"Then I stood up to get out of the truck. My right foot hurt so bad I thought it was broken. I looked down and there was blood all over my foot. Then I realized the blood on his face was from my foot - when I was kicking him I got shot! I found out later that two of my toes had been shattered. Looking down and seeing the injury, I realized how badly it hurt. But there was so much adrenaline pumping through me that I could still stand. I looked back towards the rear of the truck to see if it was on fire. There was about a six foot hole in the tanker trailer, fuel was spewing out everywhere, and a small fire was building inside the trailer and on the tires.[227]

"I turned and looked towards the front of the truck, down the bridge. But before I turned my head all the way toward the front, something hit me in the chest. It hit so hard it felt like Sammy Sosa hitting me with a bat. It knocked me off of my feet, back into the truck. As I laid there, I looked down and saw a round (bullet) buried in the vest on my chest

[224] Walsh.
[225] Walsh.
[226] Walsh.
[227] Walsh.

smoking. It smelled awful. I pulled it out of my vest and it burnt the hell out of my hand. I pulled myself back up and got out of the truck. I looked down the bridge in front of my truck and saw two little kids on the bridge, about a hundred to a hundred-fifty meters away. They both had AK-47s; one kid was about ten years old and the other was about seven. The seven-year old was holding his weapon upside down by the magazine, and the ten-year old was firing three rounds at a time at me. His first round hit the driver's side windshield on the truck - right next to my head. I turned around to grab my gun, and when I did, he shot me two more times in the back; the rounds went through me and into the cab of the truck.[228]

"It infuriated me as he kept shooting me. I grabbed my weapon, jumped out, and fired two rounds over their heads; I didn't want to shoot them - they were just l'il kids. After I fired over their heads, they turned around and ran down the bridge. Then I fell down onto my hands and knees; I couldn't breathe or move. I had been shot four times! I looked over to where my driver had been lying down - he was gone. I looked back and saw him running behind the truck, the opposite direction from where we were supposed to go. There was no way I could stop him, he was just running frantic. So it was just me on my hands and knees at this point, all alone. I couldn't breathe nor move, and my head was pounding very hard. I knew it was over with; there was no way I was getting out of there alive. I would either die or be captured.[229]

"I still was not going to give up though. I got up, grabbed my weapon, and walked over to the guardrail to look down on the highway. I stood there looking at all of our trucks blown up everywhere; the whole highway was scattered with our semis and our civilians. There was fire and black smoke everywhere. It was horrible. The last I remembered, there were two vehicles left on the highway, but I didn't see them anywhere, so I figured they had been blown up also. While I was standing there looking at the destruction, about twenty or thirty rounds hit the guardrail next to me. I fell backwards and lied down. Then I started low crawling towards the end of the bridge in the direction we were originally going. Bullets followed me the entire way.[230]

"Then, to my chagrin, I realized I was headed the wrong way on the bridge - into the middle of the city (Baghdad). I was just going to get shot again, and I probably wouldn't be so lucky the next time around. Bullets were striking all around me as I got up and ran back towards our burning truck. It sounds crazy, but at the time that was the safest place. On my way back, the last semi I had originally seen on the highway started coming up the bridge from behind our truck. It was almost demolished. All of the tires had been shot out, the trailer was burning, and it had bullet holes everywhere. It was losing fuel in multiple places. The tractor was completely trashed because of all the bullet holes.[231]

"It slowed down just enough so I could jump up on the side. I jumped up on the steps of the passenger side and told the driver to speed up. There was a driver and passenger

---

[228] Walsh.
[229] Walsh
[230] Walsh.
[231] Walsh.

inside the truck, both civilians. The driver was wounded, but not badly. The passenger (Hamill) was hyperventilating; he had been shot in the right arm."[232]

Hamill's tractor had slowed to a crawl of five to ten miles per hour as it neared the exit ramp. Hamill saw the first tanker flipped on its right side with its cab crushed. Hamill wanted to stop and check on the driver, but if he did his rig would have blocked the exit for the trucks behind him. As they turned onto the ramp, they began to fishtail. Hamill shouted, "Nelson, we can't block this ramp. Try to get over to the guardrail as far as you can. If we spin out by the guardrail maybe another truck can still get by."[233]

As they reached the top of the ramp, another truck swerved off the freeway, cut in front of them, and made the left hand turn onto the overpass. There was another tanker system that appeared to have been hit by an RPG (most likely Walsh's) and flipped over against the guard rail. Hamill's truck began to cross the bridge past the disabled truck. About a hundred yards ahead of them, the fuel truck that had just passed them was speeding up and exploded shooting flames 200 feet in the air. By then Hamill's truck was making very little progress. Just then a Soldier ran up, jumped on the running board on the passenger's side and wrapped his arm around the mirror. Hamill remembered that the Soldier yelled, "We've got to drop this trailer."[234]

Nelson yelled, "We are losing air pressure, must have happened when that big explosion hit us, must've knocked out our brakes." They dragged the fuel trailer like an anchor.[235]

Walsh claimed, "I continued to stand on the side of the truck as we went only about twenty-five to thirty miles per hour; there were no tires left on the truck, it was driving completely on the rims. As we entered Baghdad, I fired into the city buildings and just about everywhere trying to keep the suppressive fire down. Unfortunately, it wasn't working. The more I fired, the more rounds were fired at us. And I couldn't stabilize my weapon; I was attempting to hold onto the truck with one hand while firing with the other. I decided I would be more stable on the hood of the truck."[236]

Hamill remembered, "He was standing up on the running board and had absolutely no protection. He was shot in the arm but kept firing away and trying to hold on. A couple of times he grabbed another clip, bumped it, and slammed it in his M-16. He was sweeping his gun back and forth and firing, not really picking his targets. He realized he needed a better prone position. Using as a rest, he continued firing at anything that moved. We steadily crept along, barely moving at all."[237]

Walsh continued, "I grabbed the side mirror to get up on the hood, but the mirror broke off. As I was falling off, the passenger had enough sense to grab the handle on the back

---

[232] Walsh.
[233] Hamill, *Escape*.
[234] Hamill, *Escape*. Hamill thought that the Soldier was SPC Gregory Goodrich. This is where Walsh and Hamill tell the same story.
[235] Hamill, *Escape*.
[236] Walsh
[237] Hamill, *Escape*.

of my flak jacket to keep me on the truck. Since he was hyperventilating, I don't have any idea how he did it.[238]

"I tried again. I reached back, grabbed the truck's passenger window, pulling myself back up onto the truck, then I jumped up onto the hood and lied down. I fired left and right into the city. There were people everywhere with weapons firing at us, it was horrible. I have no idea how I did not get shot. I heard a weapon fire really close to us, closer then the others, coming from my right side, which was the driver's side of the truck. I looked over and saw the two little kids that were on the bridge earlier, they were firing at me again. The older one, who had shot me earlier, was firing at the trailer and the semi, and the younger kid was firing two to three rounds at a time directly at me. I fired another round over their heads but they didn't budge, and apparently they were not about to. Then I aimed at the younger kid's chest and fired the round. It went into his throat and out the other side, and he dropped to the ground dead.[239]

"The older kid looked down at him, then up at me, and started laying into it; firing twenty to thirty rounds at a time at me. I rolled over, trying not to get hit, then I aimed at his head and shot, but I missed and it went over his head and hit the wall. Luckily it knocked enough debris down on him to drop him. I knew he wasn't dead, but he was down on the ground and that was good enough for me.[240]

Hamill remembered, "We were coming up on one of the trucks that had exploded, and it was still blazing. Nelson yelled, "We can't go by they truck. We'll catch fire, too." Their tanker was spilling fuel from both sides, but they could not stop since they were still taking small arms fire. Nelson added, "This truck's fixin' to die. It's fixin' to quit." Their truck finally ground to a halt.[241]

Walsh added, "Then the truck started slowing down more and more until it came to a dead stop. I rolled off the hood and lied down in front of the truck. As I lay there, I realized all the bullets that were being fired were landing around me. A couple of strays were hitting the semi where the two civilians were. I knew that if a round hit them, they would not make it; they were already in bad shape. I got up and ran away from the truck, about fifty to seventy-five meters, and lied back down. I fired into the buildings wherever I saw anyone. At that time, to me everyone was the enemy except my own.[242]

Hamill wrote, "We had no more choices. We had to bale. Right then a Humvee pulled around in front of us at about 100 feet and stopped. Then [Walsh] rolled off the hood of our truck and fell to the ground, picked himself up, and ran for the Humvee. Nelson was running right behind him."[243]

---

[238] Walsh.
[239] Walsh.
[240] Walsh.
[241] Hamill, *Escape*.
[242] Walsh.
[243] Hamill, *Escape*.

Walsh said, "I looked back at the truck and saw the driver getting out. I knew if he got out, it would draw attention to him and he would end up being shot. I started yelling, telling him to get back in the truck, but he wouldn't listen. I know I should not have done it, but I aimed and shot a round into his door handle. I knew I would not hit him, and I hit where I intended. He jumped back into the truck and shut the door. They both sat there looking at me. I hope they didn't think I was going to shoot them. I was just trying to keep them safe.[244]

"We were stuck there for about ten minutes when a Hummer appeared coming towards us from the bridge. It was the Hummer I had seen earlier. That Humvee was our last chance. I jumped up and flagged it down. I helped the two civilians out of the semi and into the Hummer, then I jumped in.[245]

SFC Groff's armored HMMV gun truck, driven by SPC Lamar with SPC Pelz firing the SAW, had been the 21st in the original line of march. It began losing power as it drove through the gauntlet of fire and smoke and slowed down to last. Fisher's bobtail raced ahead then pulled off to the far right and he climbed out of his tractor. SFC Groff stopped and his crew pulled the screaming Fisher into the back. His left side was drenched in blood. Lamar then drove off trying to avoid guard rails and giant rocks placed in the slick road while receiving gun fire. Their HMMV continued to lose power. They picked up a couple more KBR drivers then PFC Goodrich and continued onward.[246]

When SFC Groff's HMMV HMMV reached the overpass on shot out tires, they came up upon Hamill's truck then stopped. Nelson had climbed out of his cab and was running right behind Walsh. They dove through the right door right. Hamill ran as fast as he could, wounded and loaded down with body armor and Kevlar helmet, but was about ten feet from the HMMV when it sped off. He hollered but they did not hear him. Nelson yelled at Lamar that he had left Hamill behind.[247]

Walsh added, "We took off towards the north gate of BIAP Safety. We were still about three miles away though. It was a long shot, and the Hummer had been shot up pretty badly. We drove a little ways and picked up two more people; one soldier, Gregory Goodrich, and a civilian. I was sitting behind the driver, and so when Goodrich jumped in he sat on my lap, and the civilian jumped in behind the passenger. We were really packed into the Humvee; there were about ten people in this four-person Hummer."[248]

Hamill was left standing in the middle of the road with bullets still flying. He remembered the advice of his Vietnam veteran roommate in Kuwait, "If you are ever under fire, you get down on the ground as quick as you can and stay down." Hamill did just that. He examined his escape routes but saw several Iraqis running toward him. He

---

[244] Walsh.
[245] Walsh.
[246] March, "On the move."
[247] Hamill, *Escape* and March, "On the move."
[248] Walsh.

tried crawling toward one of the houses with his good arm. Not long after he was a captive in enemy hands.[249]

Wash continued, "As Goodrich lay on my lap, he fired out the window. Next thing I knew, I felt a thump - he had been shot. He started yelling, "ah..ah..ah..I got hit, I've been hit!" I pushed him forward so I could help him. I went into the back of the Humvee and pulled out my first aid pouch. I leaned back up to help him, but blood was coming out of his mouth and he wasn't moving anymore. He didn't make it. We were rolling about ten miles an hour at top speed. Then the Humvee died, I believe it had been shot in the radiator. It was not going anywhere. We were still about two to three miles from the gate, and we were under heavy fire. There was no time in this entire attack that we were not under small arms fire, RPG's, or IED's (improvised explosive devices)."[250]

Groff's HMMV was only 500 to 700 meters from the safety of the cavalry barricade when a round through the radiator finally stopped it. Pelz saw insurgents moving up to trees all around them and began firing at them.[251]

Walsh remembered, "We sat in the back of the Humvee looking at each other. We all knew we were not going to make it. The passenger [SFC Groff] used the radio to call for help, but no one was answering. It was hopeless. We just sat there listening to the bullets bounce off the hummer, hoping no RPG's hit us, since it would certainly be all over over then. But we all knew it was already over; the Hummer was our last hope and now it was out of commission, and it was too dangerous to try and run for the gate. We sat there for about ten to fifteen minutes."[252]

SFC Groff tried calling anyone on either the SINCGARS or KBR radio then SGT Blankenship answered on the KBR radio that a couple tanks were on their way. Pelz looked up the road and saw tanks emerge from the compound.[253]

Earlier, PFC Church had rallied the cavalry troopers to mount a mission to rescue his fellow drivers then escorted them into the kill zone. Two tanks and two HMMVs pulled up. Church recognized the assistant commander's HMMV amidst heavy black smoke and flaming wreckage of burning fuel tankers. The Bradley Infantry Fighting Vehicle and up-armored HMMVs raced to SFC Groff's disabled vehicle to find two wounded soldiers and four wounded KBR drivers. They set up security around the vehicle while the enemy fire rained in from both sides of the road.[254]

Walsh claimed, "Then we heard a loud screaming like a banshee. Three of us stood up and looked out the roof of the Hummer. We saw a Bradley tank coming towards us, it drove into the city firing at anything that moved, and two more tanks were following

---

249 Hamill, *Escape*.
250 Walsh.
251 March, "On the move."
252 Walsh.
253 March, "On the move."
254 Church SSM citation.

behind it. They pulled up on both sides of us, and two armored Hummers pulled up in the front and back. They boxed us in for security. It was cool as hell![255]

"The soldiers got us all out of the back of the broken-down Hummer. I was put into the back of one of the armored Hummers with three other people. We were taken up the road about a mile, and then told that we were going to be put into a tank. I got out, and along with one of the civilians, helped the civilian that was hyperventilating walk to the tank. Unfortunately, the civilian that was helping him also was shot in the back and dropped. I dragged the hyperventilating guy to the tank and went back for the other civilian, but someone else had already got him. I looked around to see if I could help anyone. Then I got in the back of the Bradley. The soldiers shut the door and it took off. There were five people counting myself in the back of the tank. Three of them were dead."[256]

While exposed to enemy fire, Church and Pelz set up a hasty triage, identifying the most serious wounded. Church then bandaged PFC Goodrich's sucking chest wound and carried him over to one of the HMMVs. Lamar saw Church put Goodrich in the back of the HMMV; his face was covers with his body armor. Lamar knew Goodrich did not make it. Once Church and Pelz had carried all the wounded over to the HMMV, it became apparent that there was no room left for Church.[257]

Church and Pelz insisted that cavalry troopers evacuate the wounded back to the casualty collection point while he waited for their return. Groff did not know they had been left behind until he reached the safety of the compound.

PFC Church and Pelz took cover in the disabled HMMVV and engaged the enemy for the next ten minutes until the recovery team returned. Once they climbed in the HMMVs and left, an RPG hit their disabled HMMV. Upon his return to the camp, Church immediately rendered medical treatment to two more civilians with minor wounds and loaded them into vehicles for ground evacuation. Before leaving the area, Church initiated a sensitive-items check and weapons sweep to prevent capture by enemy forces. In spite of the extreme danger to himself, he maintained a clear presence of mind.[258]

SFC Groff reported that he had could account for all his men except Krause and Maupin. He expressed concern about the SINCGARS in his HMMV falling into enemy hands. CPT Munz radioed 1SG Taylor to assemble a tank team to recover the vehicle. Upon their arrival, they saw 60 to 70 Iraqis dancing in celebration around it. Taylor fired an HE round at the HMMV destroying the vehicle and radio. His gunner fired into the crowd with his coaxial machinegun.[259]

<u>Lesson</u>

---

[255] Walsh.
[256] Walsh.
[257] Church SSM citation.
[258] Church SSM citation and March, "On the move."
[259] March, "On the march."

The ambush near Abu Ghraib on Good Friday was just one of many ambushes that day, but none of the convoys took as bad of a beating as the 724th Transportation Company. Several convoys on that same route turned around and headed back. The second serial out of Anaconda changed their route to ASR Vernon and Irish into ECP1 instead of Sword. Never before had any convoy in Iraq encountered an ambush this large or intense. The enemy had taken advantage of the inexperience of many of the new units that had just arrived during the March surge. The enemy tactics had once again changed introducing large scale ambushes to the war for the road. This ambush resulted in the death of PFC Goodrich and six KBR drivers. Eight Soldiers and four KBR drivers were wounded. Around seven fuel tankers and one HMMV were left in the kill zone, a little more than on third of the convoy. Many of the wounded were evacuated to Anaconda then Landstuhl, Germany. Others with minor wounds were stabilized at different camps. The 5-ton with SGT Watson and SPC Bachman missed the turn onto ASAR Cardinals and continued straight down Sword with tanker following. One KBR driver, Tommy Hamill, and two Soldiers, SGT Elmer C. Krause and SPC Keith "Matt" Maupin, were captured. SGT Krause's body was later found on 23 April and Maupin still remains missing. The KBR driver, Thomas Hamill escaped after 27 days of captivity when he heard the voices of US Soldiers outside the building he was held hostage in. Not since the ambush of the 507th had the US taken such devastating losses on any ambush. This ambush was pivotal in the history of OIF convoy operations and required changes in convoy operations.[260]

This and other ambushes that weekend caught most units and commands by surprise in spite of the warnings that the enemy TTPs were getting more sophisticated. With every attack the enemy had shown improvement. Just like in Vietnam, they would have the confidence to try and destroy an entire convoy. This convoy did, however, have five versions of gun trucks. Clearly they did not have the fire power to stand and fight with hundreds of insurgents. The last HMMV gun truck made a noble effort to rescue as many drivers as it could, yet many drivers fell into enemy hands. No convoy in the Vietnam War that had gun trucks ever had a driver captured. The gun trucks reaction was to return suppressive fire against the insurgents so vehicles could clear the kill zone. The obvious lesson was that the vehicles needed armor, the gun trucks needed more armor and fire power and the convoys needed a better doctrine.

Many Transportation Corps Soldiers performed heroically that day, but only Jeremy Church's action earned the Silver Star Medal. On 25 February 2005, Church became the first transporter since the Vietnam War to earn this award and the first US Army Reserve Soldier in OIF. Church's coolness under fire and his disregard for his personal safety saved the lives of at least 5 Soldiers and 4 civilians.

Good Friday, 9 April 2004

96th HET Company

That same day, 15 HETS of 1st Platoon, 96th HET hauled M1 tanks of Company C, 2-8th Cavalry, 1st Cavalry Division north. SFC Powell had heard on the radio that other convoys had been hit by IEDs or would receive instructions to go to another location on account of an IED. This made them alert. The MTS in LT Renina Miller's thin skinned

---

[260] March, "On the move."

HMMV did not work so she rode in the lead HET, who's MTS did work. The platoon had five MTS and five SINCGARS radios. Her driver, PVT Ronald Gallet and assistant driver, SPC Walsh, followed. They joked, "With us two in the HMMV, something is bound to happen." The 2 ½-ton with a ring mounted M2 .50 caliber machinegun was the third vehicle. SFC Samuel Powell rode in a turtle shell soft skinned HMMV with two M249 SAWs sticking out the windows in the rear of the convoy. They departed from their RON location at CSC Scania enroute for Camp Taji.[261]

Around 1130, they approached to within 3-4 kilometers of BIAP when a HET broke down. The guys were talking about lunch on the radio. They had halted for about 15 to 20 minutes before they fixed the HET. LT Miller asked if they wanted to stop at BIAP for lunch or push on to Taji, another 30 minutes away. For some reason, they chose to go to Taji. They had never failed to stop at BIAP before. It was a good place to relax, use the internet or phones. As the convoy started, they saw black smoke off in the distance but did not think anything about it. Smoke was not unusual in Iraq. Ten minutes later they saw five buttoned up Bradley fighting vehicles race past them heading south. They realized that something was seriously wrong. Normally they did not see Bradleys on the road nor buttoned up. Powell thought to himself, "What's going on?" The others asked themselves the same question. They began to make the connection between the smoke and the urgency of the Bradleys. About that time, a message came over the MTS, "MSR Sword is Red and closed. All convoys head to BIAP." The convoy was about 15 minutes away from ASR Sword.[262]

SFC Powell called LT Miller on the SINGARS and asked, "LT did you get the same MTS message?" She answered, "Yes. We're going to turn around and go to BIAP." They halted where they were. Powell switched his SINGARS to the Sheriff frequency and heard the message, "No convoys go north of BIAP. Insurgents attacking military and civilian trucks."[263]

Gallet was used to seeing lots of civilians along side the road, but this day he only saw one. She was hanging laundry. When the convoy stopped, she ran inside. At that moment he realized things had gone from bad to worse. Everyone climbed out of their vehicles and pulled security. SSG Hurd looked down and spotted an IED hidden in the carcass of a dog. He ran up yelling, "We are stopped right beside an IED. We need to move!"[264]

Powell's attention was focused on the black smoke ahead. They had coincidently stopped next to a KBR convoy driven by American and Third County Nationals (TCN), which was heading south on a northbound lane. Evidently, they had turned around and drove back down the same lane. Guard rails in the median prevented them from crossing over into the next lane. Powell ran past his convoy to look for a place to turn around. A three-foot deep ditch paralleled the outside of the highway. Powell needed a flat place

[261] Powell and Gallet interview.
[262] Powell and Gallet interview.
[263] Powell and Gallet interview.
[264] Powell and Gallet interview.

for his HETs to turn around. They were too big to turn around just using the width of the road. He could not find a place.[265]

Some MPs in HMMVs provided security above them on the overpass. The MP HMMV drove down to ask Powell what he was doing. Powell told them that he was looking for a place to turn around. They then escorted the HETs 200 meters up the road to a level spot where the HETs could turn around one at a time. Miller waited for her convoy to catch up. The KBR trucks were parked in the inside of lane and the HET convoy in the center lane both facing south in the northbound lane. The MPs returned to the bridge. As soon as all her HETs had turned around, Miller planned to drive to BIAP. Meanwhile, Powell ran back to his HMMV, turned it around where it was and fell in behind the 2 ½-ton truck after it passed him and stopped.[266]

About that time, the MPs escorting the KBR trucks pulled their HMMV right up in front of Miller's HET, blocking its path. They halted the convoy because they had learned there was an IED along side the road. This was standard procedure if an IED was spotted ahead. In a state of high anxiety, they could not rationalize that the policy was indented to prevent convoys from running into IEDs. In carrying out the policy, these MPs had halted the convoy right beside the IED and would not let them pass. Their strict adherence to the instructions endangered lives. At the same time, SGT Hurd jumped out of his truck and jogged up to Gallet's HMMV yelling, "You stopped us next to the IED!"[267]

Powell called up, "What's going on?" Miller responded, "They don't want us to pass because of the IED." Powell could not believe what he was hearing. They were deliberately parking the convoy right next to the danger instead of letting them pass. Powell said, "We will go around them."[268]

Miller's lead HET had to back up to drive around the MP HMMV. The other trucks had to do the same to give Miller room. SPC McEndree, the driver of the 2 ½-ton truck, climbed out of his truck and walked back to make sure he had enough room behind his truck to back up. Miller saw that McEndree had climbed out on the same side as the IED so she climbed down from her HET to warn him. At the same time, they started receiving a small amount of small arms fire. A TCN driver jumped out of his truck and pointed in the direction of the firing making a gesture with his hand to indicate shooting. The KBR drivers yelled at him to get back in his truck. Just as he started to turn, the IED exploded. Shrapnel from the IED hit the machine gunner of the 2 ½-ton in the back. It exploded just as Miller and McEndree had turned around to run back to cover and blew McEndree airborne into the ravine along side the road. Miller and McEndree were both hit by increasing small arms fire from the east side of the road.[269]

---

[265] Powell and Gallet interview.
[266] Powell and Gallet interview.
[267] Powell and Gallet interview.
[268] Powell and Gallet interview.
[269] Powell and Gallet interview.

Powell was standing outside his HMMV with the handset to his ear when the IED went off. He immediately notified Sheriff that he needed a medevac and helicopter gunships. An Apache gunship arrived on station within two to three minutes and the pilots talked with Powell on the Sheriff frequency. They circled high overhead and claimed that they could not see any enemy to engage. The enemy fire continued.[270]

Powell then passed the word to his drivers, "We've got to get these tanks off loaded." The drivers and tank commanders rode in the tanks while they were chained to the trailers. The remainder of the tank crews had flown up to Taji. As soon as the ambush began, they buttoned up their hatches. The truck drivers climbed back into their HETs to maneuver the trailers so that the tanks could drive off. Powell ran up to the nearest tank and banged on the turret yelling at the gunner to put up a fight. Gallet could hear him yelling from his position several vehicles ahead.[271]

Powell then ran back to his HMMV and called the cavalry company commander and said, "Get 'em off the trucks." The commander had planned to off load just one tank, but Powell said, "You have permission to drop all of them." The commander responded, "That's what we're here for."[272]

The HET drivers began maneuvering the trailers then the TCs ran back to unshackle the chains so the tanks could drive off. SPC Bill Adkins' HET was right behind Gallet. Gallett ran back to unshackle one chain while Adkins loosened the other, all while under fire. Walsh pulled security. Gallet could hear the gun fire but did not know how close it hit until paint chips from the tank fell on him. He thought to himself, "Just get the shackle off." His focus on undoing the shackle kept his mind off of the enemy fire.[273]

Once they freed the tank, SSG Wardale, the driver of the HET, called Gallet forward to treat the wounded. Gallet was the combat life saver. He ran to the most critically wounded person first, the TCN driver. The wounded man's helmet was blown off. The man had taken the blast in the front and was punctured by shrapnel. The metal was still hot and he had not started to bleed. His left arm was also dislocated and twisted around like a contortionist. Gallet bandaged him up. As soon as Wardale had left his truck, a mortar round landed on his trailer destroying the M88.[274]

Wardale ran over to Miller and jumped on her to cover her from fire. He then yelled for help. She was still conscious but had received two wounds to her lower back. Wardale then jumped up and pulled her in between the MP HMMV and her HET. The MPs came over to help. Wardale then ran over to McEndree, who was just trying to stand up. The round had penetrated his left side, but the flak jacket deflected it back into his body. Wardale wrapped an arm around McEndree and helped him to the casualty collection point between the MP HMMV, lead HET and lead KBR truck.[275]

---

[270] Powell and Gallet interview.
[271] Powell and Gallet interview.
[272] Powell and Gallet interview.
[273] Powell and Gallet interview.
[274] Powell and Gallet interview.
[275] Powell and Gallet interview.

While all this happened, the tanks rolled off of the trailers. The cavalry commander's tank was the first off of the trailer. He was up behind the .50 caliber blazing away. He drove his tank down the median to flatten the guard rails so vehicles had more room to maneuver. The second tank backed off into the ditch and got stuck. The third tank threw its right track. The driver climbed out of his tank and looked at the broken track, then threw his Kevlar helmet at the tank in rage forgetting that he was under fire. Powell yelled at him, "What are you doing? You are getting shot at." The tanker realized his peril then took cover. To Powell the tanks drove around in confusion and circled around the disabled tanks to provide protections. The commander told Powell that they had just crossed the border and this was their first action.[276]

Two medevac helicopters arrived and Powell talked them in. The severe casualty helicopter landed on the southbound lane and the other landed in front of the MP HMMV on the northbound lane. Two more Apache helicopters also arrived.[277]

Gallet, SPC Cruz and the two MPs lifted the stretcher with the TCN and carried him fifty yards ahead to a gap in the guard rail, then across the median to the severe medevac helicopter. They climbed back over the guard rails. By this time the shrapnel in Rivera had cooled down and his wounds started bleeding. A medic from the medevac helicopter came over and pulled Rivera's flak vest off and laid him face down on the stretcher. Gallett and picked up one end of the stretcher and the two MPs the other end and they carried Rivera over to the helicopter.[278]

By this time the insurgents were firing at them from the east, north and west. The white van that Powell had seen to the east side of the road was then north of him heading west. He realized that it was dropping off insurgents. Since the MPs blocked the south, the insurgents surrounded the convoy from the other three directions.[279]

Powell saw a military fuel tanker racing down the southbound lane on rims leaking fuel behind it. The tires had been shot out. A 5-ton truck followed behind it. They stopped in the other lane a little behind Powell. They were the trucks from the 724th that had missed their turn. The Cavalry commander pulled his tank up to provide cover for the fuel tanker. The drivers of the tanker and the 5-ton jumped out, ran around and pulled the TC of the tanker out of the cab then drug him toward the casualty collection point. The MP HMMV pulled over to pick up the wounded soldier. He was already dead. The drivers raced back to their cabs, climbed in and sped off down the road. The MPs drove back and loaded the dead TC into the helicopter.[280]

After the helicopter lifted off, the KBR trucks pulled out, then the MPs drove off and with the road finally clear, Powell's convoy mounted up and drove toward BIAP. The

[276] Powell and Gallet interview.
[277] Powell and Gallet interview.
[278] Powell and Gallet interview.
[279] Powell and Gallet interview.
[280] Powell and Gallet interview.

four tanks also drove to BIAP and provided base security. Because the roads were rated black, the 1st Platoon, 96th HET remained at BIAP for 12 days.[281]

Lesson

War is chaos. When fear sets in some Soldiers are no longer capable of rational thought. When they do not know what to do, they do what they know or have been trained to do. In this case, the MPs instinctively stopped the HET convoy upon learning of the IED. The problem was that they stopped the convoy right next to the IED. They could not rationalize that the policy was intended to not let convoys approach IEDs. Their failure to rationalize endangered the convoy.

The convoy commander had several options. She could have pushed the MP HMMV out of the way and led her convoy to safety or waited. Most likely had she damaged the MP HMMV in the process, she could have been reprimanded or punished. Fear of not knowing how the senior commanders will react causes commanders on the ground to avoid conflict. This is not an unusual scenario. Some times doing the right thing in peace time is the wrong thing in war. Leaders at all levels need to know much latitude their chain of command will support them on.

During the deployment surge of March 2005, two HET convoys had been delayed by a number of unplanned events and the drivers were in need of rest. They were already at the limit of how many days they could stay out. The 7th Transportation Group had a tight schedule in order to get all combat units back to Kuwait to meet their rotation date. One convoy commander called and asked permission to rest. He was denied permission, but fearing that one of his drivers might fall asleep at the wheel, he made the decision to disobey the order. Upon receiving further information on the problem, the Group Commander directed the battalion commander to compliment the lieutenant on his decision. The other lieutenant made the same decision but did not risk asking for permission. The Group Commander relieved him of his platoon. The colonel wanted his officers to follow the protocol. The fear of superiors can exceed one's fear of the enemy.

The decision to dismount the tanks proved had great potential but the performance of most of the tanks failed to inflict heavy casualties on the enemy.

10 April 2004

96th HET Company

The increase in enemy attacks that weekend changed a lot of plans for going home. On or about 10 April, a convoy of the 96th HET retrograded the tanks and equipment of the 1st Armored Division to BIAP, but the tankers learned that their tour was extended on account of the uprising. They downloaded their tanks and escorted the 96th HET back to Anaconda to stage. The 96th HET received a mission to leave Anaconda with empty trailers to pickup another load at Camp Caldwell. Only part of the convoy went to Caldwell and the rest was locked down at Anaconda.[282]

---

281 Powell and Gallet interview.

282 Summary of interview with SGT David Romero by Richard Killblane, 8 March 2005.

The convoy consisted of four HETs, four TCNs, escorted by two HMMVs. SGT David Romero drove the lead HET with the convoy commander, SSG Postile, right behind a HMMV. An IED exploded and just missed the lead HMMV but blew out his driver side tires. Shrapnel hit the convoy commander on the head and shattered glass hit Romero in the face. The HMMV stopped and Romero fought for control of his HET to swerve around it. He brought his truck to a stop.[283]

Romero saw insurgents assaulting the convoy and he climbed out with his and SSG Postile's M-16s. He assumed that changing M-16s was faster than changing magazines. The enemy withdrew under fire. Romero then looked back at his HET. He saw the full extent of the damage to his smoking vehicle. His gas tank was peppered and leaking fuel and his trailer was destroyed. He then pulled SSG Postile out of the cab and carried him a safe distance from the vehicle, all the while watching for the enemy to return. Two TCNs came to help so Romero could return fire.[284]

About that time, a PLS convoy with a medic drove by and stopped. They loaded SSG Postile up and drove him to safety. The medic also checked out Romero. He could still drive so he disconnected the trailer and drove only his tractor. The HET trailer had caught fire.

SGT Romero earned the Bronze Star Medal with V device and the Purple Heart Medal. His wife also earned the Purple Heart during that war. They are the second husband and wife team to both receive Purple Heart Medals in the same conflict. The first was a couple during Operation Restore Hope in Somalia. Both were wounded by the same mortar round that impacted in a sleeping hanger. Romero's convoy was not the only one hit that day.

10 April 2004

227th Transportation Company (Medium Truck)

The 3rd Platoon, 227th Medium Truck Company convoy had spent three to four days in BIAP because the roads were black. The convoy had equipment bound for the US Marine camp near Fallujah. MAJ Mark Greene was the convoy commander. SFC Polee Love was 56 years old with 33 years in the US Army. He had just ridden on his first mission north. At 1545 on Saturday, 10 April, the day before Easter, his convoy of 14 M-915s carrying supplies for the US Marine left for Camp Milam, near Fallujah. The Marines provided 13 gun trucks, which consisted of nine to ten armored HMMVs, LMTVs and a 5-ton gun truck. The convoy headed north on ASR Irish.[285]

They saw burning fuel tankers but kept on driving. A mile after they reached MSR Tampa, the convoy received small arms fire from the left side of the road then spread to both. For the next ten miles, the ambush consisted of daisy chained IEDs mortars and small arms fire. The convoy lost one truck. The .50 caliber machinegun in the HMMV

---

283 Romero interview.

284 Romero interview.

285 Summary of interview with SPC Shareese McPhee by Richard Killblane, 8 March 2005 and summary of interview with SFC Polee Love by Richard Killblane at Camp Arifjan, 12 March 2005.

in front of SPC Shareese McPhee's truck jammed. The Marine dropped down and came up with an M-16 and returned fire.[286]

SFC Love called in the contact and two helicopters flew down the road. Suddenly, he felt something like a wasp sting in his right leg. He reached down and grabbed the copper jacket of an AK round and pulled it out. A few seconds later he felt a sting in his left leg. He reached down and pulled back a bloody hand. Evidently, the round had passed through his left leg and stopped in his right.[287]

SFC Love called and told the convoy commander that he was hit. MAJ Green then told Love to stop. Love responded, "Hell, no. We're getting shot at." He continued driving for about 10 to 15 minutes then started to lose consciousness. He fell over with his hand still on the steering wheel. His TC, PFC Donzie Haynes, grabbed Love and moved him out of the driver's seat then took his place all while driving at 55 mph. That woke Love up then he reached down and picked up a bandoleer. He cut the strap and made a tourniquet around his left leg to stop the bleeding.[288]

While the convoy was still in the kill zone, it slowed down. A TCN driving a white truck drove past McPhee and stopped. The HMMV gun truck in front of McPhee also stopped blocking her way so she had to stop. The TCN driver was wounded. Another TCN truck came up and stopped on the left. Since the convoy traveled down the center of the road, McPhee was boxed in. She climbed out of her truck to pull security. Meanwhile the rest of the convoy ahead of the Marine HMMV had driven off. She thought, "Oh shit." While under fire, she ran over to the white truck with the wounded TCN driver to move it out of the way but could not drive it. The other TCN driver on the left also started to move his truck. A Marine told her to get back in her truck. Her TC had taken her place as the driver. As soon as she climbed in the passenger side of the truck, the last half of the convoy drove off. They received small arms fire for 8 more minutes.[289]

When they arrived at Camp Milam, drivers pulled Love out of his truck. McPhee saw SFC Love and TCN driver. Since she was a combat life saver, she treated Love. They took him to the TMC tent. He was the only US driver wounded in the convoy. The TCN died of his wounds.[290]

Love remained there for two days then flew to the CASH at Anaconda. By that time, he was able to walk around. Evidently, it was a clean wound and there were no complications. There were 11 wounded soldiers at the CASH and the medical personnel would not wait on them. Love asked then to come in and change his bandages but they would not. He complained and they sent him back to Navistar. Love asked to go back to the APOD. Once there, the medical staff at the APOD wanted to send him to the medical hospital in Landstuhl, Germany, for further treatment. Love refused to leave and wanted

[286] McPhee interview.
[287] McPhee and Love interview.
[288] Love interview.
[289] McPhee interview.
[290] McPhee and Love interviews.

to rejoin his soldiers. MAJ Greene sent Love down to Doha for treatment and he remained there for four and a half weeks.[291]

As it turned out, the round had touched the artery in his right leg and cauterized it. Had it punctured, he would most likely have bleed to death. Love had carried a box of Johnson and Johnson Handiwipes in his left cargo pocket and the round entered it first. He believes that the Handiwipes slowed down the round just enough to save his life. He also joked with the doctor that the wipes had also cleaned the round when it entered his leg. SPC McPhee was submitted for the Bronze Star Medal.[292]

Lesson

The drivers praised the US Marines for their performance. The Marines had a reputation for following the instructions given them. They had to get the convoy through. They stayed with the convoy and did not run off to fight the enemy.

Easter Sunday, 11 April 2004

Battle of BIAP

1487th Transportation Company (Medium Truck), 812th Transportation Battalion

The defense of the south wall of Baghdad International Airport (BIAP) was not a convoy ambush. It was a battle fought by truck drivers to defend their perimeter. The action of 1LT McCormick and his crew would be the same as they used during convoy ambushes. It was this action that heightened his reputation.

That same day as the 5 April ambush, SSG Gruver had to lead a convoy of the 1st Platoon, 1486th Medium Truck from Navistar to BIAP. He listened to the reports of attacks and had a feeling something bad would happen on that convoy. He approached 1LT James McCormick of the 1487th TC, "I would really like you to go. I've got a bad feeling. I hear you kick ass." McCormick went to his company commander to ask permission to augment Gruver's convoy. CPT Patrick Hinton said, "James, you just got wounded. You should stay back, rest and recoup." James had heard the reports too and knew that the convoy was going to get hammered on the roads going up and back. He assumed that the roads would be rated as black and the convoy would get stuck out there, so he wanted to be with them. He talked with his commander a little longer. "Let me go, sir." Hinton relented and let the lieutenant pick his own crew.[293]

McCormick picked Brian Noble as his driver, SPC Brandon Lawson as the radio operator and SGT Anthony Richardson. SPC Blue Ralph, from the 812th Battalion staff, volunteered to go. He had an infantry background so McCormick let him join them. That gave him the Zebra a crew of five.[294]

30 minutes before they were to leave, McCormick visited SGT Peacock, of C Battery, 201st FA (West Virginia National Guard), and said, "I need a .50 cal worse than a dead

[291] Love interview.

[292] McPhee and Love interviews.

[293]. Telephone conversation between 1LT James McCormick and Richard Killblane, 18 April 2005.

[294] McCormick telephone conversation, 18 April 2005.

man needs a casket." Peacock responded, "Well, yeah buddy, I'll give you one of ours. Pull it over to the shop." They drove the Zebra over to the shop and cut out a hole in the turtle shell top where Peacock's mechanics installed a pedestal mount for the M2 .50 caliber machinegun. They also found some old Kevlar ballistic vests and hung them over the doors for added protection. Because McCormick was the only member of his crew who had any real experience on the .50, he manned it.[295]

Three gun trucks escorted the convoy. SPC Holloway drove the lead HMMV gun truck with SPC Brian Coe, SPC Justin Miller and SGT Tracy Dyer as the gunners, fourth in line of march. This HMMV had ballistic armor and ballistic glass. The Zebra drove in the middle of the convoy as the floater. It moved around the convoy and blocked traffic. A M915 had a gun box constructed on the back with a Mk19 grenade launcher.

On 8 April, SSG Gruver's convoy of the 1486th TC was enroute to BIAP. Around 1900, the lead elements of the convoy turned off of MSR Tampa toward the gate. The passengers of Holloway's HMMV gun truck could see the gate. Dyer sat on the left side, Coe stood in the middle with the SAW and Miller sat on the right side of the gun truck. Coe pointed to the right and said that he could even see one of Saddam's' palaces. Dyer and Miller looked over Coe's shoulder to see the palace when they heard SSG Gruver yell over the SINGARS, "Contact of the right side."[296]

After the first few vehicles of the convoy had made the turn onto the service road, they heard two loud explosions in front of the convoy. SSG Martin and Elaine F. Coleman, in the same vehicle, saw a mortar round land in the median then they received small arms fire. Coleman called on the handheld radio that they were taking fire from both sides of the road and SSG Martin started returning fire. Dyer, Miller and Coe turned around and grabbed their weapons. An estimated 30 insurgents laid an L-shaped ambush. The enemy hit in the ditches concealed by the reeds on both sides of the road. A vehicle with insurgents waited further up on Tampa under the overpass and the enemy had a mortar was concealed behind it.[297]

SPC Holloway's gun truck pulled into the left hand lane to race to the intersection to provide cover. Dyer saw three Iraqis, with weapons dressed in black, running off to the left towards cover. Dyer fired his weapon at them and they received return fire from the left and front. A round severed Coe's thumb and he fell down into the vehicle. Delaney immediately went to work treating Coe's wound. He yelled to Holloway to get to the gate because Coe needed medical help. As the HMMV began to roll forward, a round hit Dyer in the right triceps and twice in the right forearm. As they turned down the service road to Gate 7, a round hit Miller in his left arm. He fell down but stood back up to fire, all the while cursing at the enemy. Dyer also continued to fire their weapons. A mortar round landed on the left side next to the HMMV and shrapnel peppered Dyer from his

---

[295] McCormick telephone conversation, 18 April 2005 and "518th Gun Truck."

[296] Sworn Statements, DA Form 2823, Dec 1998, SSG James D. Martin, 8 April 2004; SPC Robert A. Delaney, 9 April 2004; SPC Elaine F. Coleman, 4 June 2004; SPC Stephen D. Heinmiller, 4 June 2004; SGT James Dyer, 10 June 2004.

[297] Sworn Statement of Martin, Coleman, and Dyer.

right wrist to his shoulder and hit Coe in the arm and face while he was lying down in the vehicle. As Dyer had nearly expended all the ammunition in the drum of his SAW, a round penetrated his right forearm and exited his elbow causing his arm to go limp. He could no longer hold his SAW. He moved his left hand back to fire his weapon when another round hit the hand guard. He could not hold the weapon to fire it and fell back into the HMMV. As rounds pummeled the gun truck, a ricochet hit Dyer behind the right ear knocking his head forward. Miller continued to fire his weapon until they reached the safety of the compound.[298]

Gruver had led the lead elements of the convoy to safety while the gun trucks drew and returned fire. Once in BIAP, he set about trying to get a Quick Reaction Force (QRF) out to kill zone. A TCN driver had halted his vehicle blocking the remainder of the convoy. The drivers of the first trucks to reach safety were waiting for their wounded comrades. SSG Stewart, SPC Keith Miller and PV2 Suter cut his Kevlar vest off and searched for many wounds. SSG Stewart treated the more serious wound in the arm. He also inserted the IV. All the while, SSG James D. Martin talked to Dyer the entire time to calm him.[299]

1LT McCormick noticed three cars with Iraqis driving up and down the convoy firing at it. McCormick ordered his HMMV to turn into the fire and move to the intersection. He had to jump up on the top of the HMMV since there was not room in the hole cut out to turn the .50 and fire at the cars. A round came through the mount and hit him in the hand and another hit his sappy plate knocking him down into the floor of the Zebra. He looked up and saw two insurgents walking toward his HMMV with grenades. McCormick had dropped the ammunition because his hand was bloody so he grabbed the first thing he could, a flare, and fired it at the enemy. It started a fire in the brush and caused the enemy to flee. He then grabbed his M16 and exchanged fire with them, dropping both of them.[300]

McCormick then climbed back behind the .50 and saw the tree branches, a 1,000 yards way, move and light up every time the mortar fired. He started working the tree line with his .50 until the mortar stopped firing. He expended 100 rounds into the tree line. His radio operator, SPC Lawson, had been shot in the leg and the tires of their HMMV shot out. The Zebra drove off of the road and continued to return fire while they called for the Quick Reaction Force to arrive. After 20 minutes of fighting, the QRF still had not arrived. They arrived as the fight was nearly over, just after the crew of the Zebra shot up a blue car that sped by shooting at them.[301]

The fight lasted 45 minutes and the convoy of the 1486th had five wounded Soldiers, but the insurgents lost 18 confirmed killed in action. The ambush took place a mile from the

---

298 Sworn statements of Delaney, Heinmiller and Dyer.

299 Sworn Statements of Martin and Dyer. Statement by 1LT James McCormick, n.d.

300 McCormick, "518th Gun Truck," and telephone interview with McCormick by Richard Killblane, 18 April 2005.

301 McCormick, "518th Gun Truck," and telephone interview with McCormick by Richard Killblane, 18 April 2005

gate at BIAP. A local national convoy escorted by HMMVs was also ambushed on ASR Sword.[302]

On Easter Sunday, SSG Gruver's convoy waited among the rows and rows of trucks in the gravel parking lot of Camp Flexible at BIAP for tanks to arrive and escort them to the Green Zone. At lunch time, the drivers rotated in and out of the dining facility and PX. BIAP was divided into small camps and the trucks staged in an open area near the south gate.

C Battery, 4-5 ADA, 1st Cavalry Division had responsibility for the security of the south wall and Entry Control Point (ECP) 7, which was the main gate from MSR Tampa. An 8-foot high cinder-block wall surrounded the compound. A platoon of the battery normally manned 7-8 towers with two people per tower and an Avenger HMMV on the adjacent berm. 1LT Tom Obaseki's 1st Platoon had just relieved 1LT Jason Coad's 3rd Platoon. As soon as Coad's platoon returned to Camp Victory where they lived, Coad dismissed them and reported to the TOC. There 1LT Trey Elrod, the XO, told him that insurgents were about to breech the wall. Coad quickly scrounged up as many soldiers he could, loaded about six to eight in the LMTV and drove to the wall.[303]

Heider was a village outside the south gate whose population had supported Saddam Hussein's palace. Further down the road was an old abandoned Republican Guard barracks. The village was politically neutral and generally very peaceful. A civilian also came up to the gate and said there was going to be large scale attack. Reports like this were common. Village was very quiet about this time, which was unusual for this time of the day. The Soldiers at the south gate had sighted a red-listed vehicle in the village.[304]

That morning, 1LT McCormick and his crew, like many others, sat around listening to reports of fighting the Sheriff frequency on their SINCGARS. On hearing that a helicopter had been shot down, McCormick looked at his map and realized that the helicopter was only five miles from BIAP. McCormick told the others, "Let me go see if they need a gun truck." They drove up to the gate but the guards would not let them out. As the Zebra returned to the staging area, its crew heard a loud explosion and saw a large cloud of dust rise up from the area where the trucks parked, 400 meters from the wall.[305]

What they heard was an M-6 Linebacker (ADA Bradley), manned by SSG Green, that had fired a 25mm HE round at the vehicle on the Red List. The Bradley manned a blocking vehicle 300-400 meters behind the drop arm of Gate 7.[306]

At 1220, Iraqi insurgents attacked the south wall near Gate 7 with small arms and rockets. Some drivers were with their trucks, others at lunch or the PX. SGT Ron Ball's 3rd Platoon, 227th Medium Truck Company had split up that day and his part was waiting

[302] McCormick, "518th Gun Truck.," and "April 9th Ambush."
[303] Jason Coad email to Richard Killblane, Subj: BIAP, Tuesday, July 26, 2005 3:47 pm, and Telephone conversation with 1LT Coad, 20 July 2005.
[304] Coad telephone.
[305] McCormick, telephone interview, 18 April 2005.
[306] Coad telephone.

at BIAP on a back haul mission. Ball was driving back to the staging yard. The drivers drove their M915 tractors everywhere around BIAP rather than walk. Before he reached the yard, he saw drivers in firing positions so he stopped. He and his TC climbed out of their tractor and took up firing positions behind it. Ball did not fire a round since he did not see anything.[307]

Gallet had just finished eating lunch and walked out of the dining facility to make a phone call. He heard explosions, which was nothing unusual at BIAP, but it was followed by mad chaos of mortars, RPGs and lots of small arms fire. Gallet ran to his truck and grabbed his weapon. He saw that a HMMV had driven up on a dirt mound adjacent the wall. The drivers on both sides had formed a "V" and opened fire with everything they had, .50 caliber, M16s and AT4s. The vehicle he saw was the Zebra.[308]

As soon as the enemy fire began, McCormick saw a dirt ramp along the wall adjacent to the guard tower which the QRF fired over. McCormick told Noble to drive to the ramp. McCormick yelled up at a Soldier in the tower, "We are ready to go, we'll get up on the berm and fire." The Soldier yelled down, "Wait a minute, wait a minute." Suddenly the guard tower came under heavy enemy fire. McCormick told his driver to drive up on the ramp anyway.[309]

Once on the ramp, the Zebra came under fire from a house on the left and from an irrigation ditch about 50 yards from the wall. McCormick saw more than 40 insurgents dressed in black running in the open as if assaulting the wall. The lieutenant opened fire with his .50 and ordered his crew to get out, take up positions and return fire. CPL Richardson, SPC Lawson and SPC Ralph immediately dismounted on both sides of the HMMV and returned fire. McCormick fired off 100 rounds of his .50 in less than a minute. He thought that if he could lay down enough fire, the attack would slack off. Instead, he received a hailstorm of enemy fire. The rounds passing overhead sounded like a storm of hornets had been stirred up from their nest. The situation looked bad. McCormick looked over his shoulder and called for more help but saw some Soldiers running away. After 15 minutes of fighting, SFC Haggard, from 1st Platoon, 1487th, drove his M-915 gun truck up pulled up to the right of the ramp. It had a higher platform, so he could almost see over the wall. Haggard climbed up on the wall, identified targets and directed fire of the Mk19 gunner. Five minutes later truck drivers from the 1486th and 1487th came up and joined them.[310]

The attack seemed concentrated on the area of the guard tower. RPG and mortar rounds hit the wall causing it to buckle. Truck drivers ran up to the wall to fight. 1SG Ronald "Ron" Partin, SGT Christopher "Chris" M. Lehman, and SGT Matthew D. Eby were sitting next to their HMMV gun truck parked next to the west wall when they heard gun fire south of them. They quickly cut their poncho shade away from their HMMV and

---

307 Summary of interview with SGT Ron Ball by Richard Killblane, 121 March 2005. Sworn Statement of 1SG Ronald L. Partin, 20 June 2004.
308 Powell and Gallet interview.
309 McCormick, telephone interview, 18 April 2005 and email June 1, 2005.
310 McCormick, telephone interview, 18 April 2005 and email June 1, 2005 and 30 July 2005.

donned their ballistic vests. 1SG Partin organized the other drivers into a defense. Lehman climbed into the gun turret and began loading his Mk19 while Eby drove their HMMV gun truck up to the wall. When they arrived, they saw 1LT McCormick's HMMV pulling up on the ramp then he opened up with his .50. SSG Stewart's gun truck also joined them.[311]

SGT Thomas "Tom" R. Butler, Jr. was returning from lunch when he heard the small arms and mortar fire. He ran to his HMMV where SSG Stewart, SGT Hernandez and SPC White joined him. They climbed in their gun truck and raced to the wall. SSG Stewart, SGT Charles "Chuck" M. Gregg and SGT Tom Butler then dismounted and ran up to the ramp next to the Zebra to fire their SAWs at the house on their left. SPC White fired his M16.[312]

The enemy reached an irrigation canal about 50 meters from the wall and the front part of McCormick's HMMV would not let him depress his .50 low enough to engage them. His SAW gunner fired into the canal instead. The lieutenant then grabbed his M-16 to also engage them.[313]

After reaching the staging area of BIAP, the HET convoy accompanied by the tanks of the 2nd Brigade, 1st Armored Division saw soldiers in "full battle rattle" in prone positions. Kahn asked what was going on. Someone told him, "Sir, the insurgents are attacking the wall." A couple mortar rounds landed in the staging area but did not hit anything. The drivers climbed out of their HETs and dropped down into prone positions. The Abrams tank pulled up to the tower nearest the gate. The brigade commander climbed up and took charge of tower.[314]

The colonel in the tower told McCormick to back off the ramp and let SGT Lehman's gun truck replace them. He wanted the Mk-19 to engage the enemy mortars. While backing off, several rounds hit the Zebra's windshield wounding the driver, Noble, in the face with shattered glass. Noble climbed out of the HMMV and fired his M-203 at an insurgent in a tree to his front. After the Zebra pulled off the ramp, SGT Lehman's HMMV replaced them. Richardson treated Noble's wounds. McCormick had fired 500 rounds of .50 caliber ammunition and the Zebra had been hit 14 times that weekend. After 30 minutes of fighting, he was exhausted. He saw his men laugh and cry in the same minute. Those were the side effects of adrenaline.[315]

SGT Eby and Lehman saw a number of insurgents maneuvering from a building approximately 75 meters to their left to behind the mounds of dirt along the irrigation ditches about 100 meters from the wall. They saw a mortar tube at that berm. SGT Butler directed Lehman to fire at the mortar position which was protected behind a wall

[311] Sworn Statement of 1SG Partin, SGT Christopher M. Lehman, 20 June 2004, and SGT Matthew D. Eby, 25 June 2004.
[312] Sworn Statement of SGT Thomas R. Bulter, Jr., 22 June 2004, and SSG Thomas G. Stewart, Jr., 16 April 2004, and McCormick email June 1, 2005.
[313] Telephone interview of 1LT McCormick.
[314] Khan interview.
[315] Sworn statement by SGT Lehman, SGT Eby and McCormick.

of sandbags. He fired 10 to 15 rounds and destroyed the sandbags and mortar. After five minutes of firing, Lehman yelled that he was out of ammunition so Eby crawled on top of the HMMV and helped him load a second box into the tray. Eby informed Lehman about another mortar he saw at a berm 300 meters away. By that time, McCormick and Noble came up to the ramp and spotted a third mortar tube 800 to 900 meters away. After Lehman emptied that box of ammunition, he called down for more and Eby repeated the same reloading process. The colonel in the tower called for a cease fire. After everything went quiet, the truck drivers scanned the area for enemy. Eby and a few others began collecting magazines. The tower also shouted down that the tanks were on their way. Eby backed his HMMV off the ramp to make room for the tanks. After 30 to 40 minutes of fighting, an M1 Abrams tank replaced the gun truck on the wall and ramp. One fired its main gun at the house and worked the ground in front with the coaxial machinegun. The fighting died down after that. Eby and Lehman passed out water and Gatorade to those around them and those in the tower. They drove back to find more water and learned that water had been sent forward.[316]

Coad arrived right after hearing the Abrams fire its first two main gun rounds and saw it fire the third. He also saw tanks clustered around the main gate next to the Bradley. He dismounted and told SGT Crouthamel to take the men in the LMTV up to the wall. Coad then went to find out what was going on. At that time, the two towers were still engaged by insurgents in two houses outside the wall and along an irrigation ditch. The building to the far right was two-story and the insurgents could fire down into the staging area. Coad's battery commander and 1SG Purdue went to the ECP. 1LT Elrod tried to get the tank platoon out of the road. The 1st Platoon leader was nowhere to be found. His men claimed that he was hiding in a bunker.[317]

The LMTV pulled up and Coad quickly reinforced the first tower with an extra Soldier. Since the colonel had control of the first tower, Coad took the LMTV to the next tower, a 10 minutes to drive. He remembered that the fighting raged on the whole time. He sent a Soldier up the second tower and gathered a situation report. He learned that they had counted 13 insurgents in black firing at them from the weeds. The crew of the Avenger said they had fired approximately 100-125 rounds from the M3P .50 caliber machinegun. When Coad returned to the first tower, he ran into McCormick. Coad told him to try to pull some people off the wall because things were out of control. About that time, rounds started coming from behind them. Coad ran over and told an Engineer officer to pull his guys off the wall and stop the people behind them from shooting. The tank had taken the fight out of the insurgents and the fighting had already ended.[318]

No one conducted a battle damage assessment for three days. By that time, the bodies had been removed leaving only blood trails. The Soldiers in the second tower had counted 13 insurgents and McCormick's men had estimated that they had killed 19. A local Iraqi and a boy were killed. The Soldiers on the ECP claimed that the man had run

[316] Sworn statement by SGT Lehman, SGT Eby and McCormick email, June 1, 2005.
[317] Coad telephone conversation.
[318] Coad email and telephone.

out of the house with his boy shooting. The Soldiers had admitted killing four cows, one by a tank sabot round, but the village claimed they had killed 13.[319]

Lesson

According to the truck drivers who witnessed it, the gun trucks beat back a determined enemy attack. The story of the gun trucks on the ramp circulated among the truck drivers and became legend. The guard towers only sent three reports of mortar and small arms attacks during the period from 1220 to 1305 hours. In the context of the fighting that continued across the Suni Triangle around them, few paid any attention to this fight. It was not even a blip on the radar screen of battles that weekend. Few drivers knew who the gun trucks belonged to but they credited them with saving BIAP from being overrun that Easter Sunday.

The attack on the south wall at BIAP resembled a convoy ambush in that the wall happened to protect trucks. Several gun trucks were in the area, but only one reacted immediately. The Zebra held off the attack for 15 minutes before other gun trucks rolled up to assist. As greater fire power was brought to bear against the enemy, the attack was defeated. The fight at the wall reinforced 1LT McCormick's reputation and his concept of how gun trucks should perform. He was sorely disappointed by the lack of participation many other drivers.

Easter Sunday, 11 April 2004

Ambush at Iskandariyah

172nd and 1486th Transportation Companies (Medium Truck)

Northbound convoys were significantly aware of the increase in enemy attacks on convoys around Baghdad. A convoy made up of 44 vehicles of the 172nd and 1486th Medium Truck Companies along with 43 vehicles driven by foreign nationals hauled the equipment of the 1st Cavalry Division back up to the Green Zone. Around 30 of the trucks belonged to the 172nd TC. Four armored HMMV gun trucks of the 172nd TC escorted M915s and TCN drivers of white trucks. CPT Petropoulos managed to get those HMMVs armored through a "drug deal" with a friend at Camp Arifjan. Kuwiat-based companies were lower on the priority for add-on armor to Iraqi-based units. CPT Amanda R. Gatewood, of the 172nd TC, was the convoy commander. SFC Richard "Rich" A. Bartlett was the NCOIC of the 1486th TC drivers, but SSG Aaron Brown asked to be the convoy commander of the 1486th trucks, but CPT Gatewood refused. The 1486th TC had arrived in country ahead of the 172nd and was instructed to pass on their experience to the new arrivals. Brown may have misinterpreted this guidance. Gatewood was not the best qualified TC officer to lead a convoy and Brown seemed intent on undermining her authority. Many of the wounded from the 9 April ambush were from the 1486th. The awaiting convoy also learned that there was a credible NBC threat within 25 miles of the area that they would have to drive. SFC Bartlett gave classes on and distributed chemical detection paper to each driver and conducted training in battle drills. CPT Gatewood rode in the lead armored HMMV with SSG Steve LeClair. Because of

[319] Coad email and telephone.

his superb land navigation skills, SSG Brown selected his to be the lead M915 in the convoy.[320]

The convoy of 87 vehicles had to rest over night (RON) outside of Scania the night of 10 April. They departed at 1345 hours the next day up MSR Tampa with the escort of MPs. Because the insurgents had blown several bridges and overpasses, the convoy had to take a detour onto ASR Cleveland through an urban area. Two miles after they made their turn, the MP advance party halted and warned the convoy that they had received fire further ahead. SSG LeClair and Gatewood came to the same conclusion. He said, "We can't turn around," and she replied, "Let's push on." Bartlett calmly relayed that information to the rest of the convoy. He also knew that any attempt to turn the convoy around would lead to devastating results, he decided to continue on. The convoy proceeded with caution and made the turn at a crawl onto ASR Jackson toward BIAP. Two miles ahead the MPs halted and did not proceed any further. The convoy sped up as they reached town of al Iskandariyah one mile further. LeClair rammed into the civilian cars to get them off of the road.[321]

At 1430 hours, as the convoy drove through the town, insurgents on both sides of the road opened fire with small arms, mortars and RPGs. The insurgents fired from the yards, corners and roof tops of buildings. IEDs exploded next to LeClair's HMMV. The enemy fired mortars at a low 45 degree angle at their HMMV, shredding the driver's side tire. SGT Anthony Hernandez, the machine gunner, kept the RPG gunners pinned down while SSG LeClair "hammered down" on the gas pedal to speed ahead of the convoy. They cleared the kill zone before the HMMV came to a halt. Their HMMV received a lot of small arms fire and LeClair admitted that if he did not have the add-on armor, they would have been killed. The second HMMV gun truck, in the middle of the convoy, raced to the front as soon as it learned that the lead gun truck was disabled. The third gun truck and the last gun truck remained in their original positions in the middle and rear of the convoy. All placed suppressive fire on the enemy. Hernandez was shot across the arm, but continued to fire his .50 caliber machinegun. His was the only HMMV gun truck to run along screening the convoy.[322]

SPC Lloyd drove the lead HMMV gun truck, while SPC Delaney fired his Mk19 from the ring mount and SSG Steven G. Wells kept the rest of the convoy informed of the actions of the insurgents while firing his M16 out the window. Wells selected a floating rally point two to four miles outside of the town. He positioned his HMMV so as to pull security and block southbound traffic from driving into the kill zone. The rest of the convoy followed through the cross-fire as both the drivers and assistant drivers fired out of their trucks.[323]

---

[320] Narrative recommendation for the award of the Bronze Star with Valor to SFC Richard A. Bartlett and interview with CPT George Petropoulos and SSG Steve LeClair by Richard Killblane on 5 May 2005.
[321] SSG Aaron Brown, "Supplemental Narrative for Awards, 11 April 04 – Iskandyria, Iraq." Sworn Statement by SPC Brandon E. Sallee, 11 April 2004 and Narrative of Bronze Star to Bartlett.
[322] Interview summary with SGT Anthony Hernandez by Richard Killblane, 8 March 2005.
[323] Sworn Statement by SPC John D. Delaney, 16 April 2004; and Narrative of Bronze Star to Wells.

An RPG penetrated the Conex of SSG Rich Bartlett's load narrowly missed the oxygen and acetylene bottles by a foot or two. Shaken by the possibility of the explosion, Bartlett and SPC Brandon E. Sallee continued through the kill zone. An RPG hit the front Conex of SSG Carter's load but it was a dud causing it to bounce off and land in the median. Delany, the MK19 gunner in SSG Wells' lead gun truck fired at the rocket and caused it to explode. An RPG did disable a truck driven by a driver from the 172nd. SGT Heather M. Blanton and SGT Kirk W. Brown stopped their truck long enough so that the dismounted driver could jump on the running board and exit the kill zone. Signd Mahamd, from Pakistan, hauled two M113 APCs with two Soldiers from the 1st Cav. An RPG hit his truck, tore out his hip and caught his cab on fire, but he kept on driving out of the kill zone. At the lead edge of the kill zone, his truck came to a halt; he finally fell out of the burning vehicle.[324]

As soon as SGT Ronald "Ron" C. Hicks and SPC Andrea Motley's truck turned onto ASR Jackson, they heard an explosion followed by small arms fire on both sides of the road. The kill zone spread out from the turn to the town. Motley drove through the kill zone firing both directions and came upon a foreign national crawling away from his burning truck. Motley pulled his truck up in front of the other and halted. Hicks dismounted and to treat Mahamd's wound. The two 1st Cavalry Division Soldiers provided covering fire while Hicks then drug Mahamd out of the way of passing trucks. Hicks then bandaged the leg wound. SPC Michael P. Shugrue pulled up and stopped. As the convoy commander, SSG Brown rode in an M915 bobtail in the middle of his convoy. He came upon Hicks and jumped out to help load the Pakistani driver into his cab while Shugrue dismounted and pulled security.[325]

SSG Jeffery A. Drushel with SPC Colby Leonard as his assistant driver drove the middle M915 in the convoy. Drushel saw LeClair's disabled HMMV ahead just outside the kill zone. He stopped his truck where it did not impede traffic, then both dismounted. Drushel ran forward to provide covering fire while the LeClair changed the tire.

SSG Brett A. Baxter and SPC Joanna Kim came upon a disabled white truck and observed that the driver was still in the cab. They stopped and helped him into their cab then drove off. As they drove on, they saw the disabled truck belonging to SSG Zaremba and SGT Mullen. Baxter stopped to see if they needed help but did not see anyone in the cab. An RPG hit the M915 driven by SSG Zaremba and SGT Mullen. Both were slightly wounded and the rocket set their truck afire. They abandoned the vehicle. They received enemy fire and SPC Kim returned fire on the right side. They also stopped to help, but were told to drive on to the rally point. They drove forward continuing to engage the enemy. Meanwhile, the two cavalrymen jumped into the seat vacated by

---

[324] Narrative from SGT David Boron, Narrative recommendations for the award of the Army Commendation Medal with Valor to SGT Kirt W. Brown and SGT Heather M. Blanton.
[325] Sworn Statement by SGT Rohald C. Hicks, jr., 11 April 2004 and SSG Aaron B. Brown, 14 November 2004, Narrative recommendation for award of the Army Commendation with Valor to SGT Ronald C. Hicks and SSG Jeffery A. Drushel.

Hicks. Hicks reassured Motley that he would be safe and Brown and Motley's trucks drove off.[326]

SSG Charles M. Schrack and SGT James Dominguez followed checking out each disabled vehicle to make sure no drivers were left behind. They arrived in time to see SSG Brown and SGT Hicks load the Pakistani driver in Brown's truck. Schrack stopped his M915; Hicks jumped in next to Schrack and began firing at the enemy while they drove off. They stopped near some MPs pulling security. SSG Schrack jumped in a HMMV to go back and to recover disabled vehicles.[327]

SPC Thomas F. Shaw drove the last M915 in the convoy. He had to negotiate around the damaged vehicles in the kill zone, while returning fire and maneuvered his truck so as to prevent civilian traffic from entering the kill zone.[328]

At the rally point, the trucks formed into a box formation; the drivers dismounted and took up firing positions from behind their vehicles. The NCOs checked for casualties and ammunition status. Baxter pulled up, dismounted and took charge of the box. He placed the drivers in a 360 degree perimeter while receiving sporadic small arms fire. He calmly waited at the end of the box for the rest of the truck to catch up. His calm demeanor spread to the other drivers. SPC Kim treated the wound of the foreign national in their truck then placed him in a foreign national bobtail. The insurgents were aware of the practice of forming a box several miles down the road and had prepared a second ambush. Ten minutes after the trucks started forming a box an orange civilian dump truck with a mortar drove to within 1,000 meters of the rally point from the left side of the northbound road and fired rounds into the box. Delaney fired 40mm grenades from his Mk19 and scared the assailants away. Without waiting for the remainder of the convoy to arrive, the drivers mounted up and pulled out. SSG Rich Bartlett made the decision to halt at FOB St Michaels, since not all of the trucks had caught up. St Mikes was a US Marine base. The ambush lasted around 45 minutes.[329]

The Marines sent out a QRF and counted 29 enemy killed by the drivers of the convoy. They also reported that the insurgents had mortar positions dug along the dirt road that ran parallel to ASR Jackson. The convoy lost four TCN vehicles, two green trucks and only two TCNs wounded. Hernandez was also the only American in the convoy wounded. He received the Bronze Star Medal with V device.[330]

CPT Gatewood did not seem to know what to do. LeClair asked her for the Alpha Roster so he could get an accountability of the drivers. He lined the drivers up and called out the

---

[326] Sworn Statement of SSG Brett A. Baxter, 14 November 2004., and Accident Report/Serious Incident Report, 812th TC BN, APO AE09304, Camp Navistar, Kuwait, 12 April 2004.

[327] Sworn Statement of SSG Charles M. Shrack, 14 November 2004 and Hicks.

[328] Narrative recommendation fro the Award of the Army Commendation Medal with Valor for SPC Thomas F. Shaw.

[329] Sworn statement of Delaney, Sallee, Brown and Narrative from SGT David Boron and Narrative of Bronze Star to Wells, Narrative recommendation for the Award of the Bronze Star with Valor to SSG Brett A. Baxter.

[330] Hernandez interview.

names with each Soldier responding when his name was called. When he asked those to raise their hands whose names had not been called, ten raised their hands. He realized that the roster was incorrect and he would have to question the Soldiers to determine if any one was missing. The camp commander of St Michaels asked CPT Gatewood if she had all her Soldiers accounted for. She did not know for sure. The colonel was livid. He informed her that if she was a Marine, she would be on the next plane home. Keep in mind that the Marines had suffered badly in the press when a young Marine died in the desert because the company commander did not know he was missing at the end of the training day. There was no inter-service rivalry. The Marines provided the Army convoy any help they wanted. While LeClair took his wounded Soldier to the aid station, the Marines changed all the tires on his HMMV.[331]

Meanwhile, their commander, CPT Petropoulos, was riding in a convoy 30 minutes out from Navistar when his truck master called him about the ambush. Gatewood had reported the incident to her company by MTS and the truck master informed both his commander and the battalion Commander. Petropoulos was on the returning convoy and had four other convoys north.[332]

SGT Shane Wilson drove the tenth M915 in a 100 vehicle convoy of the 172nd Medium Truck southbound from Camp Anaconda during the Easter ambushes. It had 20 to 30 Strykers as escort. Wilson's M915 was the tenth in the line of march and right behind a white truck driven by a TCN. The convoy drove at 25 mph because of the Strykers. The convoy commander told the escort commander that they needed to move as fast as they could. They were driving at 50 mph when they ran into the ambush. The IEDs exploded in the center of the convoy and a TCN driver in front of Wilson stopped splitting the convoy in two. Wilson and the rest of the convoy did drive around the TCN. Wilson could see and hear small arms fire. He radioed ahead then was knocked out by an AK round that hit his helmet. He slumped over with his hand still on the steering wheel, while they were still moving. His TC woke him up and put his helmet back on his head. They caught up with the rest of the convoy. Wilson climbed out of his truck and ran back to the Stryker for treatment. Firing began again. The infantry wanted to put one of their own men in the truck to replace Wilson as the driver, but his TC took his place. The convoy rolled into Scania.[333]

Lesson

Legends had been created. Drivers would recount the act of heroism of the truck drivers that defended the wall at BIAP. In particular, they described the heroic defense by a lone black and tan striped HMMV, the Zebra. Similarly, rumors spread about Gatewood's performance. Rumor's claimed that she had left drivers in the kill zone. This claim was unfair, for the mere fact that although she was the convoy commander, she was not in charge. Two senior NCOs had to make all the decisions. While there was talk, no one wanted to come out and outright call her a coward, but she had definitely not had a good day.

---

[331] Interview with Petropoulos and LeClair.

[332] Interview with Petropoulos and LeClair.

[333] Interview summary with SGT Shane Wilson by Richard Killblane, 8 March 2005.

The Army has an identity crisis with its warrior ethos. Senior leaders had their values shaped during a time in the feel good Army of political correctness and stress cards. That was in strict conflict with the warrior ethos. While a colonel would end the career of a lieutenant for making the right decision without asking for permission, the Army as a whole avoids the issue of cowardice. Gatewood's performance was not the only officer's performance that was questionable during this war. The Marines, however, have never violated their core values and minced no words on the subject. Because of her lack of personnel accountability they told her, "If you were a Marine, you would be on a plane home." They sent an email message to CPT Petropolous that if he ever sent her north again on another convoy, they would kill her. He made a deal and hid her in the newly formed 518th Combat Gun Truck Company. She would get a second chance to lead a convoy and would abandon a HMMV gun truck broken down on the road near Safwan at night, a place known for criminal attacks on vehicles. Interestingly, the commander of the HMMV crew was 1LT McCormick.[334]

April 2004

Green Zone convoys

1486th Transportation Company (Medium Truck)

That Easter weekend, the insurgents had dropped about five bridges blocking the MSR through those areas. They overran both An Najaf and Al Kut and blocked the alternate supply route. The vast number of ambushes caused the movement control authorities to close down the roads and code them black. The convoys were locked down until authorities considered the roads safe. The enemy had shut down the supply line. Tanks were diverted from quelling the uprising to escorting what was considered the most mission essential convoys.[335]

The 1st Cav claimed that they needed their containers urgently delivered to the Green Zone. The Green Zone was an enclosed area of Baghdad where the 1st Cav had taken up residence that was considered safe. The afternoon right after their defense of BIAP, SFC Haggard and 1LT McCormick had to go on a convoy with 14 flat beds of the 1486th and 1487th carrying mission essential cargo. SFC Haggard was the convoy commander. The 1st Cav led the convoy with two tanks out the north gate.

The loads on the flatbeds of Gatewood's convoy were considered mission essential for the 1st Cav and convoy crowded St Michaels, so the Movement Control Battalion decided to let her convoy continue to BIAP. The MCB kept delaying the departure time until Wednesday morning. The convoy pushed on to BIAP without incident. After they reached BIAP, 1st Cav tanks and Bradleys escorted them on local runs to the Green Zone and other camps to drop off their loads. The drivers became frustrated to see some of the containers stored away or learn that some of the APCs could not run and other APCs had to tow them off. The drivers had risked their lives to learn that their loads were not that important after all.[336]

---

334 Interview with Petropolous

335 Interview with Petropoulos and LeClair, and MG Stutlz, 7 August 2005.

336 Interview with LeClair.

Commander CJTF-7, LTG Ricardo S. Sanchez's obvious response to the uprising was to close the roads to convoy traffic. BG Scott G. West, J4 for CJTF7, informed his commander that they only had five days supply of fuel on hand. They came face-to-face with the reality of the concept of on-time delivery. It does not work when the opposition is determined to kill your drivers. Sanchez had to face the reality that he had to divert combat units from attacking the enemy to protecting the convoys. While most convoys were locked down for as many as ten days, the fuel trucks had to run.

The ambushes shut down the roads for weeks except for priority cargo. The ratio of gun truck to prime mover was established at 1:5 after the ambushes. On 15 April 2004, Task Force Baghdad, made up mostly of the 1st Cavalry Division, assumed responsibility for Baghdad and its environs from the 1st Armored Division. After the retrograde was complete, the gun truck ratio would return to 1:10.

17 April 2004
Ambush at Ad Diwaniyah
1175th HET Company

> AMBUSH at AD DIWANIYAH
> On 17APR04 at approximately 1715hrs, I Captain Thomas Jerry(HUD) Moore II, was leading the first of 3 HET march units into the city of Ad Diwaniyah. The march units was in order as follows; 1175th,2123rd, and 1452nd, all National Guard Combat Heavy Equipment Transportation, (CBT HET) company's. The 1175th is from TN, 2123rd KY, and the 1452nd North Carolina. We had all three loaded elements of the 2/37, 1AD from AL KUT. Our mission was to relocate 2/37 AR to FOB Duke, NLT the AM hours 18APR04 Vic Najef. Captain Peterson would be the serial commander and I would lead the first march unit. Our route would take us into the southern portion of Iraq which intelligence had said there had been very little activity going this route.
>
> We SP AL Kut around 1230 17APR04. We arrived just south of CSC Scania around 1530hrs. We had with us scouts from the 2ACR, 1st Squadron, Apache Troop. There was some confusion about the route we would take between the scouts, CPT Peterson, LT Henderson and myself. As we stopped just south of Scania, CPT Peterson sent two of the scout vehicles to go to MCT to verify the route and get coordinates. After about 30 minutes, the scouts returned stating they had the approved route and had the maps in their hands. Out front of the 1st march unit would be Apache 2, lead by SSG Vancleeve, followed by Apache 1, lead by 1LT Schuh. I radioed LT Henderson, call sign Saber 25 to notify him we were ready to move.
>
> We rolled out around 1600 hrs heading S. on ASR Orlando. As we entered into the town of Ad Diwaniyah, we came to a traffic circle and I was told to halt there by the Apache elements. They had told me there was a tractor and trailer turned over blocking our route and would take some time to clear up. The scouts left out to recon an alternate route for us. After about 10-15 minutes, they returned saying

they had found us an alternate route to just follow them. The city had looked like all other city's I had visited. The gas station adjacent to where we were sitting had cars lined up out in the road waiting to get in. Kids were running around playing soccer and beginning to come up to us asking for food and water. One little kid that looked to be about 7-8 years old told me we were going to Najef. I thought that was very strange how this young kid knew where we were headed. I been in country 366 days and had never seen this before. I radioed back to my elements and Saber 25 that we had to go around the accident ahead and we was moving out.

As we was getting deeper into the city I noticed a group of around 60-70 men gathered around along side of the road we was on. They was dressed in black, all appeared to be listening to one guy who was addressing them through a mega phone. He was quite upset you could tell by the way he was addressing them. He just did not look friendly so I relayed back on my singars for everyone to keep there eyes on the group as they came by because they just did not seem like they wanted us there. We continued on and made a left turn down street that looked more like an alley. There were low power line cords hanging across the ally from house to house. The first 2 Het's was making their way down the ally being cautious not to tear down the lines. Again things was looking normal, kids was running out lining the streets waiving at us. There seemed to be an unusual amount of adults coming out standing on the side walks. I radioed and told everyone that they seemed to be friendly and try not to tear down their power lines. Traffic was moving very slowly and I had an uneasy feeling being in this ally with these HET's as there is no room to maneuver if something happens. The adults were getting restless with us taking our time being there and began to come into the ally motioning for us to roll on and not to worry about tearing down the lines. I began to look more closely at the lines trying to figure out why they would want us to tear down the lines. The lines were very small wire and not really ran to any source of electricity as I could tell. I again got on the radio and told people to just roll on that they did not mind us tearing down there lines. This seemed so strange to me. By now you could see the adults gathering the kids up and going into the buildings. I kept looking forward hoping we was about to come back onto our ASR. We came to a traffic circle and took a right heading back down another ally. I radioed for my first gun truck to set a traffic control point there to make sure everyone made the correct turn there as there was actually 2 right hand turns in the circle. Apache elements were still in front of me leading the way. The ally in which we were traveling in was lined with apartment buildings on both sides of the road. There was no one walking in the area at this time. As we approached the end of the ally coming to a T intersection there was what seemed to be 10-15 rounds fired from what seemed to be my right. I radioed contact right, contact right. The lead HET, Tango #1 radioed there was contact left. It sounded like a large volume of fire had erupted to my rear as everyone was coming on the singars stating they was receiving fire. I had pictured in my mind that I was through the kill zone and the guys behind me were caught towards the last intersection. I radioed for Apache to go to the ambush site to help neutralize the situation. From where I was sitting the 3 HET's back, I could not see anyone in the buildings nor did I see any muzzle flashes coming from the buildings. Tango #1 came back on the radio and said one of the crewmen on the tank he was hauling was KIA and said we needed to move. By now the 50-cal gunners on the M-1's and M-88's was laying down heavy suppressive fire into the buildings. Tango one said he was at an intersection and did not know which way to go. I radioed for one of the Apache elements to come back to the front to get us out of there. You could here gunshots being exchanged everywhere by now and everyone throughout the convoy was radioing me confirming they was being attacked. I knew then we were in an ambush. Apache moved forward making a right hand turn. We went about 50 yards and came to a low overpass that the HET's could not get under and we stopped again. You could still here and see the engagements of friendly and enemy forces. We made a right and went down a very narrow ally paralleling the bridge we were halted at. This brought us out to a 4 lane road. With Apache back in front, Tango one made a U-turn heading out of town across the bridge. As I approached the bridge and made the U-turn, I heard my maintenance element Wrench #1 radio and say he was separated from the convoy and did not know which way to go. I told him to stay in place and tell me what he seen around him. He was at the last traffic circle. I could tell by now there was separation in the convoy and I was afraid people was going to start going in every which direction. I positioned my truck on top of the bridge which was elevated hoping that the HET's when they came out of the ally would be able to see me.

We were still taking fire from all directions. Each tank's crewmen were pouring massive amounts of fire into the buildings with their crew serve weapons. Some of them fired their main guns into the buildings knocking out personnel firing RPG's. No matter how much fire was coming into the buildings the insurgents kept firing. I knew that stopping the convoy was going against every piece doctrine and training I had every received. I could tell that everyone was very excited as they should be and I was afraid they would start to go in every which direction and I would never be able to get them out of the city alive. I came over the radio and told everyone I was sitting on the bridge and that I was not going to leave them unit everyone could at least see the convoy. The 50-cal gunners in all the tanks and track vehicles was putting on an awesome display of fire power in conjunction with the individuals in the trucks that was having to shoot and move fighting for their life. I could also hear on the radio the coordination and movement of my 4 gun trucks. The gun trucks repeatedly put their lives in danger going back and forth laying suppressive fire until all vehicles had cleared what appeared to be three kill zones. It was hard to sit on top of the bridge because my men were hollering that we had to move that they were still receiving fire from the front to the rear. I again called on Apache to go back into the fire fight to help facilitate getting the convoy back together so we could move. I heard Wrench #1 come over the radio telling wrench #3 to make that right that he could see the tail end of the convoy. I then felt like I had everyone going in the right direction and we could move out.

Apache came back to the front and we began to roll further out of town. We went around one traffic circle and then came to a T intersection. I radioed and asked if we were all together and wrench #1 came back and said they had caught up to the convoy. He also said he had the 2123rd element with him. It was about this time Saber 25 came on the radio and announced his LT, 1LT Henderson had been hit. I switched my radio over to both the sheriff and medevac frequency but could not raise anyone. I radioed my NCOIC Warrior #2 SSG Lee that was bringing up the rear. I told him to keep calling for medevac that I could not get them. I realized I had to stay on my frequency to stay abreast of the situation. I told Saber 25 they had to keep moving. SSG Grimes who was with Saber 25 in a calm manner radioed back and stated he needed a medevac immediately. We made a right at the T intersection and crossed over 2 bridges. I looked ahead for the possibility of us getting attacked again. We passed through an Iraqi checkpoint and there was a clearing with just a few houses about 1200 meters off the both sides of the road. I told Apache we had to stop and set up a perimeter. I ordered the front trucks to set up the box formation blocking both sides of traffic so no one could get near us.

Saber 25 called on the radio again as we pulled into the box pleading for me to send someone back into the city because his trucks was stuck down there. I immediately exited my vehicle and motioned for the front tanks to dismount. The commander of the tanks, Battle 5 was riding on the tank on my vehicle. I told him I needed for him to send some tanks back down into the city to help get everyone out of there. There were some tanks that took time to unchain their tanks and others that just gave the gas to the M-1 breaking the chains and running down the ramps heading into the city. I can honestly say every tank crew was out on their tank wanting to go back to the fight. I called out on the radio notifying everyone that I wanted a casualty collection point set up at the front of the box formation. Warrior #2 had gotten in touch with medevac and they were in route. Saber 25, SSG Grimes told me he was now in charge of the 2123rd element and asked very calmly what I needed him to do. I told him to park his vehicle next to mine and keep me updated as to where his personnel were. I asked the Apache elements to keep trying to get air support in there as well as get a QRF responding to our location as we was still taking fire. I also told Apache #2 he needed to be looking for the route out of here that as soon as the medevac secured the casualties I wanted to move.

It was now getting dusk probably around 1900 hours. You still hear a fierce fire fight going on in the city. Realizing we was going to be in the box formation for an extended period of time, I told my NCO's to tell everyone to start getting there night division goggles out and start scanning the perimeter. There were 3 casualties brought up from the rear. The medics lead by SGT Carlson and other soldiers was trying to hold pressure on the wounds. Two of the casualties had been shot in the femoral artery and the other was reported to have a gun shot wound to the chest area. I could see LT Henderson's condition was deteriorating quickly. Being a Registered Respiratory Therapist, I could see he was crashing fast and soon would need an artificial airway if he was to survive. I grabbed Gun Smoke #1 SSG Cross and told him to take my place on the radio. I grabbed my oxygen and medic bag and ran to where they were working on LT Henderson. He was still struggling to get up but just barely conscious. I leaned down and told him who I was and what I was going to do. If I could get the air way in and give him oxygen, it would help to ensure he would not have brain damage and also help protect his lungs should he aspirate. On the other hand, if I tried to place the tube in his airway and he did regurgitate before the tube was in place, his lungs would be filled with the vomit causing him more harm. I prepared my equipment and decided I would try quickly one time. I opened his mouth and placed my larynga scope into the back of his throat, I could see where the tube needed to be but his vocal cords kept collapsing on the tube. He now started to gag and I realized I needed to stop so as not to cause further harm. I told him I was sorry and to hang in there the chopper was on the way. Minutes later I noticed they were doing CPR on LT Henderson.

I ran back to my truck to get an update on the situation. Apache #2 told me there was a Spanish QRF coming from our south and should be here anytime. He radioed the rear letting everyone know not to shoot the QRF as they would be there soon. Warrior # 2 was talking to the medevac, call sign medicine man 23 and you could here him I the area. I was still getting reports that more HET's was still entering into the rear of the formation. Battle 5 told me there was a disable HET left in town and wanted to know what I wanted to do with. I ordered to destroy it as it was not worth the risk recovering it. SFC Handy call sign Scooby Doo had now came forward and told me he was in charge of the 2123rd. I told him just to stick with me.

I told Gun smoke #1 to get his LZ kit and prepare to receive the chopper. We knew we had houses on both sides of the roads but did not see very many people stirring about the area. The LZ was marked just outside the front of my truck with chem. Lights placed on a side road. The chopper came in and as it was descending came under fire from the houses to our right. The whole entire right flank engaged the houses but the chopper had to get out of the AO. Medicine man 23 called and said he had to leave. He suggested we move the LZ further down the road. Apache #1&2 went down the road and located a safer LZ about 1 mile down the road. We notified everyone to mount up in their vehicles that we had to move down the road. The casualties were placed on an empty HET trailer and I gave the order to move out. We went about 1 mile down the road and set up another box formation to protect us. Warrior #2 called the medevac back in. The LZ was again set up by Gun Smoke #1 to the front of the formation. The chopper came in quickly sitting down at the first LZ site. I radioed for Gun Smoke #3 to run out and tell the pilot we needed him to move to the front of the formation. Within a period of 3-4 minutes the chopper was up and back down loading the casualties. No time was wasted loading them and the chopper was quickly away.

I needed another assessment as the only thing keeping us there now was getting accountability of personnel and the dismounted tanks. Someone came to me and reported there was more than 60 HET's in the formation. It was then I knew the 1452nd had followed the 2123rd and came through the ambush. I radioed for someone in the rear to find out who was in charge of that unit and have them contact myself, call sign Warrior 5 on my freq. Apache #1&2, and myself made a quick assessment as to what we had to do to move. I told all of the leaders of the units to give me an update on the status of their equipment, personnel, and ammo. The tank commander told me he had an M-1 disabled and had to download an M-88 to go back to the rear to recover it. Apache 1&2 and myself got out the maps and done a quick recon. I told him I wanted to go to the nearest coalition base to get these troops into a safe location. It was now approaching 2100hrs. SSG Grimes had now contacted me and told me he had a soldier that flew out with the medevac at a coalition base that was close to our position. I told him to get the grid coordinates. Apache #2 had also found a base that was to our North, Vic Hilla but would also but a hot spot and dangerous. The coordinates came back and we plotted them on the map. The base was just to our rear but would force us to go back through the edge of the ambush zone. No way was I asking my troops to go through there again. Our only other option was to continue on to our destination, Camp Duke Vic Najef. Apache #2 plotted a course and briefed me on the route. It was about 120 K away, which would put us getting there in the early morning hours. I told him to prepare to go this route. There was one city we had to go through. I told Apache #2 before I would move from here I wanted air support to cover us getting through the city and also contact FOB Duke to be on alert in case we needed another QRF. I then told the tank commander I wanted 2 M-1's to the front, middle and rear of the convoy in case there was anymore trouble. My troops I knew would be mentally and physically drained by now. I briefed the leaders of route we would travel and the support we would have. I knew we had to convince the soldiers they would be safe so they could concentrate on driving instead of being attacked. Leaders of the 2123rd, 1452n, 2/37 AR and Warrior #2 had came over the radio and reported they had everyone accounted for. That was amazing and probably the first sigh of relief I had received since coming under the ambush. I still feared that there was some soldier stuck in the city and the enemy would mutilate them as they had been doing in previous attacks.

It is now approaching 2300hrs. I went around checking the physical and mental status of my troops. Some are praying, others are wondering when we are getting out of there. I told as many as I could that we were continuing on with our mission going to our drop point. I described the route and the support I had for us so we would not be attacked again. I asked several soldiers if they were up to completing the mission and surprisingly not a one of my soldiers said they needed help driving. It was hard to ask them to keep driving on. 1). We were just in fire fight for our life that lasted over 1.5 hours continuously. Also they had been in a defensive position for over 3 hours. Now I would have to ask them to drive another 4-5 hours. This would put them being awake for over 24 hours.

It's around 2315hrs, the M-88 is loaded and all vehicles are either ready to move or being towed. The HET's had plenty of fuel to make the trip. We told all light wheeled vehicles to dump 10 gal of fuel to make sure they could make the rest of the journey. Maintenance from all 1175th and 2123rd had gotten all of the vehicles up in the entire convoy which was now over 70 vehicles. If not for there quick work and knowledge of the HET systems to perform temporary repairs, we would have had to stay in the defense longer than we did, putting us at risk for another attack. I sent word for every element to get on my freq so we could have commo throughout the convoy. I radioed one last status check to verify if everyone is ready to roll, Apache element ready, Battle #5 ready, Warrior #2 ready, Scooby Doo ready, 1452nd(T-Dog #1) ready. I would place Scooby Doo to bring up the rear and keep me posted as to what was happening back there. We moved out along the route as planned. All along the route you could see men carrying flags and walking along the side of the road. I know everyone had to put a bead on every person we passed as now there main concern was survival.

Things were quiet on the radio. I was afraid the troops would drift off asleep. I tried to maintain a check on personnel by talking with everyone I knew that had a radio in the entire convoy. There was a Ranger#1, Viper, and several Tango elements of my unit that would check on each other to help stay awake. Everyone was pulling together to help each other make it through this mission. As we came into the city, I could hear the air support in the air just as the Apache element had requested. That was our last choke point. I was finally feeling safe. We made one last turn heading North, only about 45 miles to go. Battle #5 calls me over the net, some of the tanks was down to 1\8 of a tank and needed to be loaded up for the rest of the movement. I put Warrior #2 and Scooby Doo in charge of getting this done. After about 30 more minutes the tanks were quickly loaded and we were again ready to move. I pleaded over the net for everyone to hang in there that we was almost there.

Finally around 0430hrs, we made a left turn and headed into FOB Duke. The sand was of fine powder and several of the HET's got stuck. We down loaded the tracks and I had one more formation to ensure one more time I had all of personnel. I then thanked them for the job they had done the last 24hrs and put them to bed down for 6 hrs. Scooby Doo had done the same for his troops. Ranger#1, Saber 25, Scooby Doo and I sat around and discussed the last 24 hours and then started planning for the next day. We came to the conclusion; this group would stay together and would always be one family and share this bond we had developed due to the unfortunate circumstances we had encountered in the last 24hours. The sun was starting to rise as I laid my head on the cot.

After reading sworn statements from members of the 1175th, it was brought to my attention that TTP the insurgents used were, IED's daisy chained together, RPG rounds and a heavy volume of small arms fire. The attack was very well coordinated.

In closing I would like to say this mission was a success due to the following:

1. The ability of all of the drivers to shoot and move. Almost every vehicle was having to fire and maneuver at the same time for an extended period of time.
2. Soldiers remaining calm during chaotic and unusual circumstances.
3. The NCO's of the 2123rd stepping forward in the absence of their fallen platoon leader.
4. The maintenance teams getting the equipment back into a condition where the trucks could safely move.
5. NCO's of all five units pulling together providing leadership and guidance to their subordinates.
6. My special Thanks to Apache #1 and #2 for all of the information and guidance they provided me allowing me to make my decisions that resulted in the mission being completed with the loss of only one piece of equipment and 3 lives were lost out of over 300 soldiers.
7. Special Thanks also goes out to Battle 5 for coordinating the mission to recover everyone out of the city quickly.
8. To all of the brave men of 2/37AR that was on this mission, if not for you and your superior fire power that you accurately directed and inflicted on the enemy, there would surely have been many more casualties. Another remarkable feat was that were only 1 piece of equipment lost during the attacks.
9. Most of all, my heart goes out to the families and friends of the three soldiers that paid the ultimate price, 17 APR04, Theatre of Iraq, Vic City of Ad Diwaniyah;

1. 1st LT Robert Henderson II, 33, 2123rd Transportation Company, (Combat HET), Kentucky National Guard
2. SGT Jonathan N. Hartman 27, 2nd BN, 37th Armored Regiment, 1Armored Division
3. PFC Clayton W. Henson, 20, 1st Squadron, 2nd Armored Calvary Regiment

Thomas J. Moore II, (Warrior 5)
CPT, TC TNARNG
XO/OPS

April Uprising Lessons

The Al Sadr uprising had run its course by the end of April and subsided under the pressure of the Marines and Army attacks. The Marines pulled out of Fallujah on 30 April and the Madhi militia turned in their weapons for money. A lull followed as the insurgents reorganized and regrouped for their next offensive. When they resurfaced, they focused their attacks on civilian targets or the Iraqi military and police in an effort to disrupt the national election set for January 2005. The threat against convoys reduced to IEDs and small arms fire. On 15 May 2004, the CJTF7 was redesignated as Multi-National Corps-Iraq (MNCI), under the command of LTG Thomas F. Metz. MNCI similarly made its plans to recapture Fallujah in the fall of that year.

The obvious lesson to the general officers in both Iraq and Kuwait was that the convoys needed gun trucks and a convoy security doctrine. Both commands agreed that convoys traveling north of Convoy Support Center (CSC) Scania could not exceed 30 vehicles and had to have a one-to-five ratio of gun trucks to task vehicles. The military truck companies would no longer provide shooters for the contract vehicles but would integrate one green (military) truck with every three white (contract) trucks for KBR convoys and one to five for Kuwait contract convoys. The 7th Transportation Battalion at Anaconda would redesignate certain truck companies as gun truck companies. The 372nd Transportation Group in Kuwait would receive the 125th MP Battalion to conduct convoy security but would also organize a provisional company from volunteers. CPT Robert Landry would recruit, organize and train the 518th Combat Gun Truck Company. He only recruited one person, 1LT McCormick. He wanted McCormick to develop the company's TTPs. Based upon his recent experience and what he learned from the infantry manual, he came up with the turn, fix and fire concept. The following was his instructions to the gun truck crews for reaction to contact.

"The first thing that must be remembered during any contact with the enemy is to maintain your composure and report the direction of contact. At the first sign of contact be it IED, RPG or Small arms fire it is important to locate the source, this can be very difficult especially in a built up area where sound will echo off of buildings and in alleys. The first sign to look for is flashes and the next would be dust and sound, you will hear fire and your first reaction must be to SCAN, once the location is determined whoever has the information must send up the report. EXAMPLE: (This is Regulator 02 CONTACT Right 200 Meters, Small Arms Fire, IED, Mortar Fire, RPG.) The use of smoke and flares on the contact side in the direction of enemy fire is also effective in helping Gun Trucks to spot the enemy. The use of yellow smoke seems to have an intimidating effect on the enemy they seem to fear it and believe it may be a form of chemical agent "GET YELLOW SMOKE". Flares seem to make the enemy nervous, at night I have seen some insurgents stop shooting to look up at the flare, make sure you shoot it at a slight angle toward the enemy fire. At this point vehicles in the convoy will proceed out of the kill zone even if they are not in the kill zone you MUST NOT STOP, push through the fire do not allow your convoy to be split up it will be a disaster. Return fire!! Effective, Aggressive fire on the enemy, the enemy you face here is much more aggressive than any we have seen they will only displace if you make them displace. Gun Trucks must not be a shoot on the go element, Gun Trucks must turn and face the contact and deliver effective fire, soldiers in the vehicle must get out of the Gun Truck using the doors as cover and delivering suppressive fire. The gunner on the top is a target, gunners should not be sky lighting themselves and they must get down behind the gun at name tape level. In the event the gunner is hit the TC must get on the gun and continue the fight. Gun Trucks must stay in the kill zone and not leave until after they have accounted for all trucks in the convoy. If you have a down vehicle Gun Trucks must maneuver into a defensive position to defend the down vehicle and make a decision to do recovery or extract driver and leave down truck behind, this decision is made by convoy commander if he is available. The destruction of abandoned US and coalition equipment has been suspended although the destruction of equipment is a long in use practice that has been written in doctrine for years, you must obtain permission to destroy and equipment you can't take with you. Actions by convoy and Gun trucks not engaged will be to move out of kill zone to move forward to a position that is varied between 2 to 5 miles remember that the enemy is very aware of the 2mile rule and most times you will run into a secondary ambush or IED at that point so push beyond that point it is also important to remember the convoy can be up to 4 miles long so the last vehicle has the be out of that 2 mile range and not the first this has caused some convoys to have the first 10 trucks out of the line of fire but still have the rear of the convoy in the kill zone, the last truck should mark the mileage. The box formation is not a difficult maneuver but when you add civilian drivers in that convoy it can be a total disaster, make sure if you are using the BOX everyone is briefed and understands how to do it prior to moving out. Ambushes are varied and in most cases they are initiated at the 4th to 10th truck back this is done to help split convoy the divide and conquer theory."

18 October 2004

518th Combat Gun Truck Company

On 18 October 2004, the 518th Combat Gun Truck Company escorted a 34 vehicle convoy from Scania to Anaconda. The 5-ton gun truck, "Heavy Metal," led the convoy with one CEP 20 trucks back and the other in the rear. SGT John O. Williams was the driver and NCOIC of 5-ton gun truck, "Big O." That 5-ton gun truck could get up to 82 mph so it could race ahead of the convoy to block any traffic. The 518th kept the gun trucks in the rear because they can accelerate faster. The convoy commander's HMMV was in the middle.[337]

As the convoy came up to the turn onto ASR Sword, "Big O" raced ahead and blocked traffic on the right side. Elements of the 1st Cav Division had the road blocked off for an IED, so the convoy stopped just short of an overpass. SGT Williams heard shots from the left rear of the convoy. So he moved "Big O" back to the rear of the convoy and fell in cover an ammunition trailer. He removed the ammunition placard so the enemy would not know which trailer had ammunition.[338]

To personnel disarming the IED. This was a new tactic of the insurgents. They would set an IED out and wait for the EOD personnel to come. Normally, the convoys would be stopped long before they reached the location of the IED. This provided an example of the detailed planning and rehearsal of the ambush and inflexible execution. They evidently did not know what to do when the convoy pulled up so they did what they had trained to do, fire at the overpass. The RPGs exploded on the overpass injuring no one.

All the CEPs pulled out onto the road between the enemy and the convoy to create a gun shield for the trucks then returned fire. "Big O" fired its .50 caliber machinegun at muzzle flashes. The ambush ended 3 to 4 minutes after it started.[339]

---

337 Summary of interview with SGT John O. Williams by Richard Killblane, 8 March 2005.

338 Williams interview.

339 Williams interview.

Lesson

The insurgents in Iraq operated very much like the insurgents did in Vietnam. They conducted detailed planning and rehearsal of their ambushes but were inflexible in the execution. They could not change the plan and take advantage of the convoy that halted in front of them. The advantage of an ambush is the element of surprise enables the ambushers to destroy targets with their opening volley. That is one reason the attackers initiate with the most lethal weapons first. After the opening rounds, then chaos reigns and the battle can go to either side. The enemy was probably counting on the fact that when an IED was spotted, convoys were usually stopped where they were. The enemy had not accounted for a convoy reaching the kill zone. The fact that the enemy was inflexible in the execution of their plan was their weakness.

The gun trucks of the 518th did exactly what they were supposed to do when halted. They pulled out and established a gun wall. They were alert and were in the perfect position to return fire when the enemy fired at the approaching HMMV. Having lost the element of surprise, the fight went quickly to the side of the 518th. It was a very one-sided fight.

The US Army tends to reward inefficiency when it comes to issuing out awards for valor. If everyone in the organization performs exactly the way they should then there is no opportunity for any one person to stand out. Only when things go wrong does the burden of success fall upon individuals. History will show that the most chaotic operations produce the most heroes. In this case, the 518th executed their reaction to ambush drill exactly as they were supposed to. Only SGT Williams earned the Bronze Star Medal with V device for using taking risk to protect the explosive cargo.

20 March 2005

Battle of Bismarck

518th Gun Truck Company and 1075th Transportation Company (Medium Truck)

See AARs

Lessons

The Anti-Iraqi Freedom Insurgents evidently liked to attack on significant dates. This ambush was launched on the anniversary of the beginning of the ground war in 2003 and also Palm Sunday. While this was not quite the anniversary of the Easter Weekend ambushes, it was close. They clearly wanted to take hostages as they had done on Good Friday 2004. Unfortunately for them, the situation turned bad for them.

This ambush also hinted that they wanted to take advantage of the one-year rotation policy of the US Army. The last big ambushes began in April 2004 when all the units were new to the theater. By March 2005, no OIF 2 transportation units were on the road. The 518th Gun Truck Company had reformed from volunteers in November of 2004, but the new leadership had abandoned the turn, fix and fight tactic and had not place the same emphasis on weapons training. This was its first big ambush. As the Army would send brand new units to Iraq each spring, the Iraqis would gain another year of experience. The individual rotation policy during the Vietnam War ensured a better transfer of knowledge and experience, it resulted in poor cohesion. The unit rotation provides better cohesion but leaves the units vulnerable during the first few months of their arrival.

The turn of events was not due to the lack of planning and preparation of the insurgents. This was a well planned and executed ambush. They managed to block all but one truck from leaving the kill zone. None of the previous ambushes had done as well. The two key factors on the side of the Americans was the determination of SPC Delancy to kill as many insurgents as he could before they killed him and the flanking maneuver by the two MP CPPs of the 617th Military Police Company. Essentially, these two actions caught the insurgents in a cross fire, an L-shaped ambush in reverse.

There were some errors on the part of the Americans though. By riding at the head of the convoy, the convoy commander was able to escape the kill zone, but was the only one. He was unable to influence the action behind him. In the event that an ambush splits a convoy, most of the important decisions have to be made in the middle or rear of the convoy. The lead element will most likely always escape the kill zone. By the end of the Vietnam War, convoy commanders knew to ride in the middle or rear of the convoys for this very reason.

The assistant convoy commander was a junior E5 and did not take action. NCOs led many of the convoys in Iraq yet none of their military education trained them for this. Instead, his driver made the right decisions and took action to rescue the wounded drivers, get the contract drivers in their trucks and clear the kill zone. By 1969, the 8th Transportation Group in Vietnam appointed convoy and assistant convoy commanders based upon their experience rather than rank. It was not unusual for a sergeant to be a convoy commander with a lieutenant riding along to gain experience.

This was the first major ambush for the new members of the 518th Gun Truck Company. This is a problem with one-year rotations. The new units have to learn how to fight the war for the first time while the enemy had two years of experience. The crews of did not perform like the original company. The lead CEP hit the breaks causing all the trucks behind it to come to a stop and bunch up. The CEP remained in the kill zone but drove back and forth rather than turning into the enemy, fixing and fighting them. The second CEP cleared the kill zone as soon as the driver was wounded and abandoned the trucks. The third CEP wanted to get into the action but used the convoy as cover as it drove up the road. Once it found a gap, the CEP peeked through, seeing a berm the CEP raced across the street for cover. While this may have been noble work for a dismounted infantry unit, it was not what was expected of an armored CEP assigned the responsibility of protecting the lightly armed cargo trucks. Delancy was furious that he did not see any CEPs protecting his M915. However, the CEP did join the MPs in time to turn back an enemy assault. This action accounted for most of the enemy killed. They ended up doing the right thing for all the wrong reasons.

The worse indictment of all CEP and CPP crews was the employment of the M2 .50 caliber machineguns. None of the .50s of the 518th could fire more than seven rounds before the weapons misfired. Clearly the head space and timing was off on all three. This demonstrated a clear lack of training and familiarization with the weapons, another change in focus with the new leadership. Even then, had the gunners been trained properly, they could have spun their barrels tight and backed off three clicks and the weapons would have functioned. When the M2 machine gunners in the two MP CPPs were wounded, no one replaced them in the turret. It reflected that thought that a weapons was assigned to each Soldier. When that Soldier was wounded or killed then the weapon was taken out of action. In infantry units, they know to always man the critical weapons, especially the machineguns. Every Soldier is trained on the operation of the crew served weapons for this possible contingency. At one point in the ambush, none of the .50 caliber machineguns were firing. The Americans had given up use of their most lethal weapons and had to resort the M16s and SAWs.

Regardless of the performance of the participants, no American was killed or captured and 27 Iraqi insurgents lay dead. That was a pretty good day in anybody's book. The previous year when the Iraqis similarly attacked new units, they did not fare as well as the units did on 20 March 2005.

In consequence of their actions, SPC Jason Mike, SGT Leigh Ann Hester, Staff Sgt. Timothy Nein and of the 617th Military Police Company and SPC Beck of the 1075th Medium Truck Company received Silver Star Medals for their actions under fire.

Conclusions

The study of convoy ambushes and counter ambush operations reveals certain patterns. Some of these never seem to change and to violate them leaves convoys vulnerable to greater losses. These are principles of convoy operations and should be made doctrine. Tactics, on the other hand, vary constantly. Immediate action or battle drills provide options to combine as tactics, but tactics should not be considered doctrine.

An ambush is an attack based upon the element of surprise. The element of surprise allows the enemy the liberty to select which targets to destroy first and the number of targets depends upon how well coordinated the fire is. A convoy ambush differs from others in that the targets are vehicles and is generally restricted to the road. In most cases, convoy ambushes are linear but depending upon the path of the road or surrounding terrain may vary.

The advantages of vehicles are that they can be armored and armed with crew served weapons and can drive fast. While the road can allow them to drive fast, other road conditions can significantly reduce their speed or even stop the convoy. The size of trucks makes them easy targets when halted or driving slowly. Being road bound, the enemy knows the path the convoy has to follow. This makes it easy to obstacle the road with road blocks or explosives.

Convoy organization

History of convoy operations during the 19th century, Vietnam and Iraq reinforces that a certain convoy organization works best. Convoys should not exceed 30 vehicles because it is easier to control, minimizes risk and does not take up enough road space to disrupt civilian traffic. The minimum security consists of right seat passengers with weapons, called "shotguns" during the Indian and Vietnam Wars and "shooters" during Operation Iraqi Freedom. The best defense consists of armored vehicles dedicated as weapons platforms. The term gun truck refers to any cargo truck used as a weapons platform. Different terms were used to avoid confusion between the larger platforms that could carry more than one crew served weapon system and smaller platforms that could only carry one. During the Vietnam War, armed ¼-ton M151s were called gun jeeps and armed ¾-tons were called gun beeps. During Operation Iraqi Freedom, up-armored HMMVs with crew served weapons were called Convoy Protection Platforms (CPP) based in Iraq and Convoy Escort Platforms (CEP) based in Kuwait. Whatever the term, history proves that they should be placed front center and rear. For simplicity, this author will refer to them collectively as gun trucks and individually by type.

If other escort vehicles are available then an advance guard and rear guard should be formed. The advance guard should consist of vehicles that can accelerate rapidly to screen the road ahead to identify potential problems in order to give the convoy commander time to properly react.

The rear guard should consist of a reaction force that can reinforce the main body and possibly flank the enemy. That is why it travels a safe distance behind the convoy.

There were a couple times during the Vietnam War where the security force had responded to a decoy ambush but were in a position to more rapidly respond to the main ambush. The rear guard can either be gun trucks or combat arms. Gun trucks are restricted to the roads and have limited avenues with which to flank the ambush while dismounted infantry or combat vehicles can do this over a greater variety of terrain. There is a danger in the rear guard consisting of infantry riding in unarmored cargo trucks if the enemy is looking for an increased body count. The infantry passengers provide the enemy a better target than the cargo or fuel trucks.

Convoy discipline reduces vulnerability. History also agrees that 100 meter interval is ideal to reduce the number of vehicles in the kill zone. Dividing convoys into serials of less than 30 vehicles further limits the number of trucks that are vulnerable and if the serials are close, allows the gun trucks from one convoy to reinforce the other.

Immediate action drills

Throughout history this convoy organization provided the best capability to protect the convoy. Battle drills provide the building blocks for tactics. Some US Marines believe that the best reaction to an ambush is for the drivers to stop, dismount and attack through the kill zone. For any military organization where the primary training is based upon the philosophy that everyone is an infantry man first, this reaction might work. There is one fundamental flaw in the concept. Dismounted infantry march with an interval of five to ten meters between them. If caught in an ambush, they are close enough to support an attack on the enemy. Vehicles ideally travel with an interval of 100 meters between them. Even if the vehicles are bunched up, the length of the vehicles does not bring the drivers close enough to mount an ambush. As seen in the ambushes on Route 19 on 2 September 1967 and at Ap Nhi, Vietnam, on 25 August 1968, the drivers had to fight as infantry but because of the spacing of the vehicles, they fought isolated battles. The similar situation happened to the 1075th Medium Truck convoy during an ambush on ASR Bismarck, in Iraq, on 20 March 2005. There is no good example of drivers beating back a well planned ambush when they dismounted and fought as infantry. This should only be a last resort. The main advantage that trucks have over dismounted infantry is that they can more speedily flee the kill zone.

What ambush after ambush during the Vietnam War teaches us is that superior and accurate firepower determines the victor. After the element of surprise is lost, the safety of the remaining vehicles and crews depends upon whether the convoy can mass superior firepower against the enemy. The question of how many weapons a gun truck must have or how many gun trucks should escort a convoy depends upon the worst case ambush scenario that the enemy can present. During a Good Friday ambush of 2004 in Baghdad, Iraq, several hundred insurgents laid an ambush for the 724th POL convoy that stretched for four to five miles. Five gun trucks with one crew served weapon each was clearly not enough. The convoy lost 7 out of 19 fuel tankers, lost seven contract drivers killed, two military and one civilian drivers captured. While this study examined the actions and results during convoy ambushes, there were claims in both Vietnam and Iraq that a well armed and well disciplined convoy deterred the enemy from attacking it. More gun trucks and weapons pointing out the openings in cargo vehicles possibly intimidated the enemy and forced them to select weaker targets. During OIF, this was called the porcupine effect. On certain occasions during the Vietnam War when the probability of attack was high, the 8th Transportation Group sent out convoys of entirely gun trucks. The enemy avoided contact with these "death convoys." During the Korean War there were a few convoy ambushes and the convoys settled on a ratio of one ring mounted machinegun per every three task vehicles. During the Vietnam War, the ratio of gun trucks was one to ten, but with three to four machineguns per gun truck the crew-served weapon ratio was close to one to three. Up until 2005 during OIF, the highest commands settled on a ratio of one to five gun trucks to task vehicles, but the requirement for each platform was only one crew-served weapon each. The logical answer to the question of how many crew-served weapons should protect the convoy is more weapons than the enemy can bring to bear against it. The deciding factor in any gun fight is superior and accurate fire power.

An ambush will occur in the front, middle or rear of the convoy either stopping the convoy or dividing it. Reaction to an ambush should consist of three possible scenarios, vehicles that have driven past the kill zone, vehicles in the kill zone and vehicles about to drive in the kill zone. Those vehicles that can clear the kill zone should continue to safety, whether it is a "floating rally point," security check point or military camp.

Those vehicles that are disabled in the kill zone have their choices narrowed. Drivers of task vehicles can dismount and take up fighting positions behind their trucks or in the cabs if armored. The drivers should remain with their trucks until rescued by passing trucks or gun trucks. Accountability is the problem. If a driver has been rescued by a passing truck escaping the kill zone then they should notify the convoy commander and gun trucks. This will prevent weapons platforms needlessly waiting in the kill zone looking for the driver.

The vehicles that have not entered the kill zone have greater choices. They can continue to drive through as did the 172nd and 1486th Medium Truck convoy did on Good Friday ambush 2004 in Iraq. The leaders based their decision on the fact that previous kill zones were only a few hundred meters long and they had the speed to race through it. Under that assumption it would have been more difficult to turn a convoy of tractors and trailers around and head back. This kill zone, however, stretched for over a mile. The decision of the 2123rd HET to take a detour around a disabled vehicle in Ad Diwaniyah on 17 April 2004 actually sent them into the kill zone.

The second choice is to halt and wait for other forces to clear the kill zone. When a convoy escorted by the 518th Gun Truck Company was halted on ASR Sword in Iraq on 18 October 2004, this placed them across from Iraqi insurgents lying in wait. Fortunately for them, the enemy was waiting for the Explosive Ordnance Demolition HMMV to drive up to disarm the improvised explosive device. Sticking to the plan, the insurgents missed the opportunity to disable a greater number of soft skinned vehicles. After they opened fire on the HMMV arriving on the overpass, five gun trucks in blocking positions opened fire on the enemy and the one sided fight ended in a few minutes. The problem with halting is that it makes the convoy a more vulnerable target. Speed is security. It is harder to hit a moving target than a stationary one. The ambush of the 96th HET in Baghdad on Good Friday illustrates that. The MPs halted a convoy right next to an IED after it had turned around, because that was their policy. The delay allowed the insurgents to conduct what appeared to be a hasty ambush. A similar thing happened to the recovery convoy blocked by the Koreans at a bridge along Route 19 in Vietnam on the night of 16 December 1970. In most ambushes during the Vietnam War, the enemy initiated with the highest casualty producing weapon on a particular vehicle or vehicles in a certain location that would block traffic for the purpose of destroying the remaining vehicles with subsequent fire.

The third option is to turn around and return to the safety of a compound where the convoy can wait. This may not always be an option if the blocked road is too narrow to allow tractors and trailers to turn around. If halted, the convoy must take up position ready for a hasty ambush. There is any number of defensive formations; however, vehicles bunched up make easy targets for mortars as witnessed ambush of the 172nd and 1486th convoy on the Good Friday 2004. The enemy anticipated that the vehicles that had escaped the kill zone would drive ahead about a mile and for a box. The insurgents were waiting for them with a mortar in a dump truck.

Whatever the drill, it imperative that everyone knows it. The drivers and gun truck crews should understand what they do in any of the three scenarios.

Tactics

While the previous discussion describes the action of convoy vehicles in general, the action of the gun trucks allows for greater tactical options. Assuming that a gun truck is an armored vehicle and dedicated weapons platform, its purpose is to protect the convoy. To do this they have to turn the fight back on the enemy as rapidly as possible through superior fire power. That means they have to they have to lay down suppressive fire until all the vehicles have cleared the kill zone and if vehicles are trapped or disabled in the kill zone, the gun trucks have to rescue the driver and defend the vehicles until the convoy commander determines to abandon the vehicles.

One question is whether to suppress enemy fire from inside the kill zone or flank. The answer has to depend upon the nature of the kill zone and enemy positions and friendly situation. If friendly vehicles are trapped in the kill zone, then the gun trucks need to protect them. By entering the kill zone and firing on the enemy, they draw fire from the other trucks. They can also use their vehicles to block explosive cargo as SGT Wells did on the 27 November 2004 ambush.

At best superior fire power beat back the enemy, but it was flanking action that prevented their escape. The 4 January 1970 ambush along Route 19 in Vietnam provides an excellent example of where the Koreans cut off the retreat of the insurgents when the accurate fire of the gun trucks drove them from their positions. Most ambushes in Vietnam ended when the reaction force arrived. During the ambush on ASR Bismarck in Iraq on 20 March 2005, two CPPs of the MPs and one CEP of the 518th drove down the access road and flanked the insurgents resulting in as many as 27 enemy killed. This flanking action clearly caught the enemy by surprise and was the decisive action of the battle. It worked because the enemy did not expect it. The problem of flanking with road bound vehicles is that the enemy can predict which roads they might try to flank on. When behavior becomes predictable, then the enemy can plan for it. The enemy can set traps for the flanking element. Flanking is best left to dismounted infantry or combat vehicles that can drive off-road.

Another question that has arisen is how aggressive the convoy security should be. 1LT McCormick believed that gun trucks should shove the fight back down the enemy's throats. This idea had supporters during the Vietnam War. Some gun truck crews felt that the gun trucks needed to turn the fight back against the enemy as quickly as possible. The mission of the Transportation Corps, however, is to deliver the men and material to their appointed destination on time. A purely defensive philosophy would only have the gun trucks remain in the kill zone long enough for all the vehicles to clear the kill zone. A defensive tactic does not discourage the enemy from further attacks but might encourage him to continue his quest to find the best ambush tactic. Turning the fight back on the enemy and making him pay a higher price in casualties would more likely discourage him from attacking again until he has learned from his mistake. Most ambushes during the Vietnam War ended with the gun trucks fixing the enemy until the combat arms units arrived and flanked the enemy. The flanking movement by the 617th MP Company during the Battle of Bismarck on 20 March 2005, inflicted heavy casualties on the enemy.

One rule should be followed, if the convoy divides never leave an element of the convoy unprotected. If the lead element of the convoy flees the kill zone, at least one gun truck should accompany that element. As seen on the ambushes along Route 19 on 25 January 1968, 8 March 1968 and 9 June 1969, the enemy employed a decoy ambush to draw off the gun trucks in hope of having the convoy drive into the main kill zone unprotected. There has to be some balance between how long some gun trucks can remain in the kill zone waiting for the infantry and its ability to respond should the convoy encounter another ambush up the road.

<u>Command, control and communication</u>

Unity of command is paramount. In convoys throughout history there has been a convoy commander and escort commander. Who does history say has authority over both? The person who understands the mission better. Because most combat arms commanders do not understand the capabilities and limitations of most of the vehicles in the convoy and think in terms of closing with and destroying the enemy, the transportation officer or NCO should have authority over both the convoy and its escort. This has been a tough pill for field grade officers of the combat arms units to swallow, but too many problems have arisen with combat arms escorts during OIF. They tend to run off and leave the convoys unprotected when contact was made with the enemy. The armored vehicles drive slowly when they should drive fast. When the two commands worked together for the common goal of protecting the convoy all the way to its destination, they were successful. Convoy commanders praised the support of the US Marines during the April Uprising in Iraq.

During the Vietnam War, it took about a year to get radios for every gun truck. Lucky convoy commanders had two radios, one to talk with the security force defending the road and another to talk with the gun trucks. The lesson of every contingency or war after Vietnam was that every truck needed some form of communications. By the April Uprising in Iraq, this was close to a reality. There was a consequence of this though. Without truck drivers trained in radio discipline or combat arms terminology, the different networks became cluttered with noise and the commanders became overwhelmed with processing the high volume of information. During the 20 March 2005 ambush at ASR Bismarck, the convoy commander was not able to talk with his subordinates because of the excited drivers talking on the radio.

By 2005, most convoy commanders had double stacked SINCGARS radios, one to talk with the military drivers and escort and the Sheriff net to talk with the units responsible for support in the area of operation. They also had either a Citizen Band (CB) radio or Motorola to talk with the KBR contract drivers and an internal head set to talk with the crew of their CEP/CPPs. During an ambush, this could easily result in information overload. During the ambush of 20 April 1971, LT Baird kept his radio transmissions brief telling the gun trucks only what they needed to know. He had total confidence that they would do the right thing. He only spoke one more time upon the arrival of King Kong, to inform the crew that the enemy had infiltrated the ditch near him. Convoy personnel need the same training in radio discipline as combat arms Soldiers, who at most only have to monitor two radio nets at the same time.

www.ingramcontent.com/pod-product-compliance
Lightning Source LLC
LaVergne TN
LVHW061224100826
845148LV00004B/850
9781780390246